P9-BZK-883

S. T. Coleridge

(After a painting by PHILLIPS)

SELECTIONS FROM COLERIDGE

THE RIME OF THE ANCIENT MARINER, CHRISTABEL, AND KUBLA KHAN

Edited

With Introduction and Notes

by

LINCOLN R. GIBBS, A.M.

PROFESSOR OF LITERATURE AT ANTIOCH COLLEGE

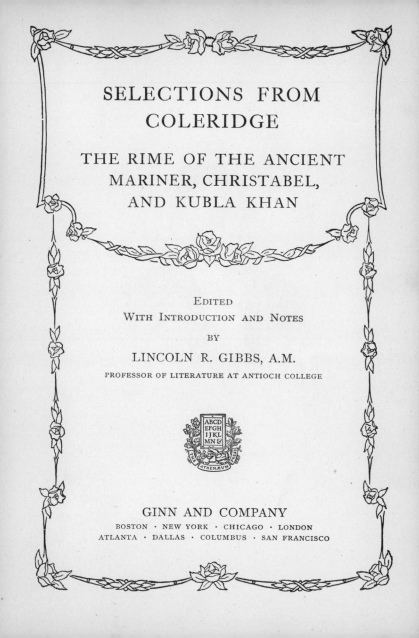

GINN AND COMPANY

BOSTON · NEW YORK · CHICAGO · LONDON
ATLANTA · DALLAS · COLUMBUS · SAN FRANCISCO

COPYRIGHT, 1898, 1916, BY
LINCOLN R. GIBBS

———

ALL RIGHTS RESERVED

323.12

The Athenæum Press
GINN AND COMPANY · PRO-
PRIETORS · BOSTON · U.S.A.

PREFACE

In this volume *Christabel* and *Kubla Khan* are added to
The Ancient Mariner, which was included in the series of
Standard English Classics in 1898. The book is by these
additions made to include the highest point of Coleridge's
achievement in pure poetry. His mastery of rhythm, his
descriptive color, — both strong and delicate, — his atmosphere, "the wizard twilight Coleridge knew," appear in their
fullness only in these three poems. Not only are they the
apex of the author's achievement; they also represent the
completion of several tendencies through which English
poetry, in the last third of the 18th century, groped toward
new forms and ideals.

But these poems do not speak adequately for their many-
minded author. To say nothing of his prose writings, his
poetry, notwithstanding its slender bulk, reveals traits of
mind and character concerning which *The Ancient Mariner*,
Christabel, and *Kubla Khan* contain scarcely a hint. To
these poems the student should add at least a few examples
of Coleridge's best work in other kinds than sheer romance,
imagination, and melody. *France: an Ode* and the *Ode to
the Departing Year* best illustrate his interest in political
liberty; the *Hymn before Sunrise in the Vale of Chamouni*
is the most impressive of the poems on nature; and *Frost
at Midnight*, *Dejection: an Ode*, *This Lime-tree Bower*

my Prison, _Work without Hope_, and _Youth and Age_ afford glimpses of his personal experience, glad or pathetic.

It has seemed proper to include in this volume only a short biographical sketch. Students whose curiosity may lead them to seek a more detailed knowledge of the poet's life are referred to the biographies by Hall Caine, Alois Brandl (translated into English by Lady Eastlake), and J. Dykes Campbell. Coleridge's own _Biographia Literaria_ is essential to a mature knowledge of his mental development.

The text of the first version of _The Ancient Mariner_ appearing in this volume I believe to be faithfully copied from the edition of 1829, with a few unimportant changes in punctuation and typography and a few readings from the edition of 1834; that of _Kubla Khan_ and _Christabel_ is from the edition of 1834. The earlier version of _The Ancient Mariner_ is reprinted from the appendix of J. Dykes Campbell's edition of the poetical works of Coleridge (London and New York, 1895). The variants printed in the notes are taken from Ernest Hartley Coleridge's edition of the _Complete Poetical Works_ (Oxford, 1912).

The full-page illustrations in this edition are made from the plates by Sir Joseph Noel Paton, R. S. A., whose series of pictures for _The Ancient Mariner_ is among the finest examples of illustrations in line.

L. R. G.

University of Pittsburgh

CONTENTS

———•◦•———

INTRODUCTION

I. SKETCH OF THE LIFE OF COLERIDGE

SAMUEL TAYLOR COLERIDGE was born at Ottery St. Mary's, Devonshire, on the 21st of October, 1772. His father, John Coleridge, who combined the offices of parish clergyman and schoolmaster, was a man of great learning, amazing eccentricity, and childlike simplicity in the ways of the world — traits which his son Samuel Taylor inherited in full measure. It is related of John Coleridge that he sometimes quoted the Old Testament to his country congregations in the original Hebrew, in order that they might hear "the authentic language of the Holy Spirit." The boy Coleridge was unnaturally precocious, being able to read a chapter of the Bible at three years, entering the grammar school at the same age, and beginning the study of Latin at six. His tastes, moreover, were not those of a healthy boy: he played little with his brothers and loved to be much alone, dreaming and reading fairy stories.

In 1781 his father died, leaving a large family in narrow circumstances. Thereupon Coleridge became a pupil of Christ's Hospital, London, a charitable institution for the education of orphan boys. The early years of his school life were unhappy. The discipline was barbarous, the slightest offenses being punished by a flogging; the food

was ill prepared and insufficient; little attention was paid
to the health of the boys.[1] Coleridge, a warm-hearted and
poetic lad, longed for his country home in Devonshire. In
Frost at Midnight, he says of his schooling:

> I was reared
> In the great city, pent mid cloisters dim,
> And saw nought lovely but the sky and stars.

But Coleridge's school days, though sometimes wretched
and lonely, were by no means idle. Indeed, his mental
growth was too rapid to be quite healthy, and even as a
schoolboy he developed the widely diversified tastes which
in later life made it impossible for him to fix upon a calling
or even to carry a literary project to completion. A visit
to the hospitals with his brother Luke aroused his interest
in medicine, and for a time he read voraciously whatever
he could find on that subject, in Greek, Latin, and English.
Before his fifteenth year he was deep in metaphysics, the
taste which he then acquired for Neoplatonic mysticism
persisting throughout his life and strongly influencing both
his philosophy and his poetry. After reading Voltaire's
Philosophical Dictionary, he professed himself an infidel,
whereupon the head-master, the Rev. James Boyer, promptly
resorted to the cane and gave the boy a flogging, the only
one, says Coleridge, that he ever deserved.

During the last two years of his stay at Christ's Hospital, Coleridge's principal taste in reading was for poetry.
The influence of Milton's descriptive poems and of Gray
may be traced in his early work. He also read with eager-
ness the sonnets of Bowles (published 1789), which would

[1] See Charles Lamb's " Christ's Hospital Five-and-thirty Years After "
(in the *Essays of Elia*).

now be utterly neglected were it not for the part they played in forming the tastes of Wordsworth and Coleridge. Whatever their intrinsic worth may be, they are at least of the Romantic school, which was about to declare its principles and gain its victories in the work of Coleridge and Wordsworth. The former professed an extravagant admiration for them, and on leaving school made forty copies of them with his own hand, which he presented to his schoolmates as parting gifts. To the present generation Bowles represents the weakness rather than the strength of the Romantic tendency, — its undisciplined emotion, degenerating into sentimentality; but to Coleridge his work was a welcome contrast to the frigid artificiality of the imitators of Pope and Johnson; it had the saving qualities of sincerity and spontaneity.

After remaining in Christ's Hospital nine years, Coleridge became a student of Jesus College, Cambridge, entering the university in 1791, just as Wordsworth was leaving it. His career there, though auspiciously begun, was a disappointment to his friends and ended disastrously. For the first year he studied diligently, obtaining in 1792 the Brown medal for a Greek Sapphic ode. Later he became a desultory student, though not an indolent one. His rooms were a gathering place for the most radical spirits in the university, who met there to discuss the stirring events of the French Revolution. Before leaving Christ's Hospital, he had celebrated in verse the destruction of the Bastille; and perhaps the most important fact in his mental history from 1791 to 1794 is the quickening of his democratic sympathies by his reading and associations at the university. Godwin's *Political Justice* came to his hands, and he became a convert to its communistic creed. He soon gave evidence of his democratic convictions in a ridiculous manner.

In December, 1793, in a fit of despondency, caused by debt and perhaps by a disappointment in love, Coleridge left Cambridge and went to London to seek his fortune. Finding himself in the city with scarcely a penny in his pocket, he obeyed a sudden impulse to enlist as a dragoon. This he did under an assumed name — Silas Tomkyn Comberbach; but after a few months of service, some Latin verses which he scribbled on his stall led to an investigation, his friends procured his discharge, and he was restored to the university.

In June, 1794, Coleridge visited Oxford and made the acquaintance of Southey, then a student at the university. A few weeks after, they met again at Bristol. Southey was full of democratic ideas, which he dreamed of putting into practice by establishing a communistic settlement on the banks of the Susquehanna. He had no difficulty in arousing the ardent interest of Coleridge in this visionary scheme. They named the enterprise Pantisocracy. Its fundamental principles were the abolition of exclusive privileges and private property, and the universal reign of brotherly love. The Pantisocritans hoped that a few hours of daily labor would provide for their needs; the rest of the time they purposed to devote to conversation and literature. They needed money to charter a ship and purchase supplies; but they were penniless themselves and could enlist in the enterprise only those whose fortunes were as desperate as their own. All attempts to raise money failing, Southey, to Coleridge's great disgust, abandoned the project and accepted an advantageous offer to go to Lisbon with an uncle.

. Meanwhile, Coleridge had left the university without a degree, and had complied with one of the important regulations of the Pantisocratic community by taking a wife. On the 4th of October, 1795, he was married to Miss Sara Fricker, of Bristol.

His opinions in politics and religion, which in youth and early manhood were heretical, had prevented his taking a degree at Cambridge and barred him from a career in the university or the church. For more than a year he had formed no other plan for the future than the impracticable Pantisocracy project. This failing him, he found himself, in the winter of 1796, with no certain means of support for himself and his wife. He settled at Clevedon, near Bristol, and tried to gain a livelihood by publishing a volume of his collected poems, lecturing, and writing for the press. In the spring of 1796 he edited a political and literary journal of his own, *The Watchman*, which failed after ten numbers, for lack of subscribers. Hoping to get a Unitarian pulpit, he preached a few times in Bath, but his eccentricity in dress and in the choice of subjects — he appeared in the pulpit in a blue coat and white waistcoat, and on one occasion preached on the Hair-Powder Tax—prevented him from getting the desired appointment. These struggles, eccentricities, and failures are typical of his entire life.

After nearly a year's residence at Clevedon, Coleridge removed to Nether Stowey, in Somersetshire. In June, 1797, Wordsworth, with his sister Dorothy, took up his residence in the neighboring village of Alfoxden, princi-

pally for the sake of Coleridge's society. Wordsworth's
Descriptive Sketches (1793) had come into the hands of
Coleridge, who saw in them the certain announcement of
a great poetic genius. Wordsworth, on his part, had been
attracted by Coleridge's lectures in Bristol. Only the
opportunity for personal intercourse was needed to create
a life-long friendship. Wordsworth shared Coleridge's
disgust with artificiality and his desire for plain living and
high thinking, without sharing his vague dreams of immediately founding an ideal community. The best of his
influence on Coleridge was moral rather than literary.
From the stronger character of Wordsworth, Coleridge
gained confidence in his own powers, purpose, and energy.
During the months when the two poets were neighbors—
from June, 1797, to September, 1798 — he wrote much
of his best poetry,— *The Ancient Mariner*, the first part of
Christabel, *The Dark Ladie*, *Fears in Solitude*, *France*, and
Kubla Khan. The years 1797 and 1798 are the culmina-
tion of his career as a poet.

In September, 1798, Coleridge again found himself in
financial difficulties. A pension from the Wedgwood
brothers, makers of the famous pottery, enabled him to
spend a year of study in Germany. Henceforth he was
no longer primarily a poet, but a critic, theologian and
philosopher. From this time forward, therefore, the events
of his personal history and even the growth of his mind
and character are comparatively uninteresting to students
of his poetry, and we may pass rapidly over them.

In 1799, upon his return to England, he began his work
as a pioneer in introducing German thought into England,
by translating Schiller's *Wallenstein*. After a period of

successful service on a London newspaper, he was offered a lucrative position as editor, which he declined, fearing that the routine duties would interfere with "the lazy reading of old folios." In 1803 the consequences of inherited weakness and of indiscreet exposure during his school days appeared in the form of a painful rheumatic affection. For relief he had recourse to a nostrum which contained laudanum, and in this way began a slavery to the opium habit, which lasted till 1816. In 1804 he went to Malta in search of health, acting as secretary to the governor, but returned to England in 1806. This period of his life (1803–1816) is the melancholy record of bondage to the opium habit, separation from his family, and genius wasted and misapplied. He supported himself by hack work for the newspapers, by lecturing on Shakespeare, Milton and the fine arts, by compiling text-books, and by writing sermons for indolent clergymen. In 1809 he made a second unsuccessful venture in journalism, *The Friend.*

In 1816 Coleridge became an inmate of the house of Dr. Gillman, of Highgate, London, under whose care he gained the mastery over the opium habit. Here he continued to reside till his death in 1834. During this period he wielded an influence which had previously been denied him. He was visited by many of the noblest and most promising young men in England — Edward Irving, Julius Hare, A. H. Hallam, John Sterling, J. H. Green, and Frederic Denison Maurice, who listened to him as to a spiritual father. Both by his conversation with this group and by his *Aids to Reflection* (1825) he profoundly influenced the religious thought of England in the direction of a liberal, practical, and spiritual Christianity.

About 1830 his health began to fail, and on the 25th of July, 1834, he died.

Coleridge's contributions to English literature, in spite of their miscellaneous character, are not without a certain unity of aim. His work in criticism, almost as important as his work in creative writing, is an exposition of the principles underlying the Romantic movement, of which he was the great critical mind. His lectures on Shakespeare — though often more enthusiastic than discriminating — had their share in promoting the revival of interest in Shakespeare which marked the early years of the century. His criticism of Wordsworth was influential in breaking down the prejudice against which Wordsworth was compelled to struggle and in hastening his tardy recognition. As a critic, as well as a poet, theologian, and philosopher, Coleridge's position in the history of English literature is that of protest against the barren formalism of the 18th century. If it were necessary to characterize him in a single phrase, he should be called the supreme asserter of the rights of the imagination.

The following are the dates of publication of Coleridge's more important works:

The Watchman,	1796.
Ode to the Departing Year,	1796.
The Ancient Mariner,	1798.
Wallenstein (translation),	1800.
Remorse,	1813.
Christabel,	1816.
Biographia Literaria,	1817.
Sibylline Leaves,	1817.
Zapolya,	1817.

Aids to Reflection, 1825.
Table-Talk, 1835.
Confessions of an Enquiring Spirit, 1840.
Notes upon Shakespeare, 1849.

II. ORIGIN OF THE *LYRICAL BALLADS*

The Ancient Mariner was first published in the *Lyrical Ballads* (1798), the origin of which Wordsworth has described in the Fenwick note to *We Are Seven:*

In the autumn of the year 1798, he [Coleridge], my sister, and myself, started from Alfoxden pretty late in the afternoon, with a view to visit Lenton and the Valley of Stones near it; and, as our united funds were very small, we agreed to defray the expense of the tour by writing a poem, to be sent to the new monthly magazine, set up by Phillips, the bookseller, and edited by Dr. Aiken. Accordingly, we set off and proceeded along the Quantock Hills towards Watchet, and in the course of this walk was planned the poem of *The Ancient Mariner*, founded on a dream, as Mr. Coleridge said, of his friend, Mr. Cruikshank. Much the greatest part of the story was Mr. Coleridge's invention; but certain parts I myself suggested: for example, some crime was to be committed which should bring upon the old navigator, as Coleridge afterwards delighted to call him, the spectral persecution, as a consequence of that crime, and his own wanderings. I had been reading in Shelvock's *Voyages* a day or two before, that while doubling Cape Horn they frequently saw albatrosses in that latitude, the largest of sea fowl, some extending their wings twelve or fifteen feet. " Suppose," said I, " you represent him as having killed one of these birds on entering the South Sea, and that the tutelary spirits of those regions take upon them to avenge the crime?" The incident was thought fit for the purpose and adopted accordingly. I also suggested the navigation of the ship by the dead men, but do not recollect that I had anything more to do with the scheme of the poem. The gloss with which it was subsequently accompanied was not thought of by either of us at the time; at least, not a hint of it was given to me, and I have no doubt it was a gratuitous afterthought. We began the composition together on that, to me, memorable evening. I furnished two or three lines at the beginning of the poem, in particular:

> And listened like a three years' child;
> The mariner had his will.

These trifling contributions, all but one (which Mr. C. has with unnecessary scrupulosity recorded), slipped out of his mind as they well might. As we endeavored to proceed conjointly (I speak of the same evening), our respective manners proved so widely different that it would have been quite presumptuous in me to do anything but separate from an undertaking upon which I could only have been a clog. . . . *The Ancient Mariner* grew and grew, till it became too important for our first object, which was limited to our expectation of five pounds, and we began to talk of a volume, which was to consist, as Mr. Coleridge has told the world, of poems chiefly on supernatural subjects taken from common life, but looked at, as much as might be, through an imaginative medium.

Of the objects of this volume, Coleridge has given a full account in *Biographia Literaria*:

During the first year that Mr. Wordsworth and I were neighbors our conversation turned frequently on the two cardinal points of poetry, — the power of exciting the sympathy of the reader by a faithful adherence to the truth of nature, and the power of giving the interest of novelty, by the modifying colors of the imagination. The sudden charm which accidents of light and shade, which moonlight or sunset, diffused over a known and familiar landscape, appeared to represent the practicability of combining both. These are the poetry of nature. The thought suggested itself (to which of us I do not recollect) that a series of poems might be composed, of two sorts. In the one, the incidents and agents were to be, in part at least, supernatural; and the interest aimed at was to consist in the interesting of the affections by the dramatic truth of such emotions as would naturally accompany such situations, supposing them real. . . . For the second class, subjects were to be chosen from ordinary life; the characters and incidents were to be such as will be found in every village and its vicinity where there is a meditative and feeling mind to seek after them, or to notice them when they present themselves.

In this idea originated the plan of the *Lyrical Ballads*, in which it was agreed that my endeavors should be directed to persons and characters supernatural, or at least romantic, yet so as to transfer from our inward nature a human interest and a semblance of truth sufficient to procure for these shadows of imagination that willing suspension of disbelief for the moment which constitutes poetic faith. Mr. Wordsworth, on the other hand, was to propose to himself, as his object, to give the charm of novelty to things of every day, and to excite a feeling analogous to the supernatural by awakening the mind's attention from the lethargy of custom and directing it to the loveliness and wonders of the world before us; an inexhaustible treasure, but for which, in consequence of the film of familiarity and selfish solicitude, we have eyes which see not, ears that hear not, and hearts which neither feel nor understand.

III. CRITICAL COMMENTS

Whether or not a born "maker," he [Coleridge] was certainly a born theorist; and we believe not only that under all his most important achievements there was a basis of intellectual theory, but that the theory, so far from being an alien and disturbing presence, did duty as the unifying principle which coördinated the whole. We think we can see such a theory underlying *The Ancient Mariner*, and securing the almost unqualified success of that poem; and we further think we can see it departed from in one isolated instance, with temporary artistic disaster as the result.

Any one examining the poem with a critical eye for its machinery and groundwork will have noticed that Coleridge is careful not to introduce any element of the marvellous or supernatural until he has transported the reader beyond the pale of definite geographical knowledge, and thus left behind him all those conditions of the known and the familiar, all those associations with recorded fact and experience, which would have created an inimical atmosphere. Indeed, there is perhaps something rather inartistic in his undignified haste to convey us to the æsthetically necessary region. In some half-dozen stanzas, beginning with "The ship was cleared," we find ourselves crossing the line and driven far towards the Southern Pole. Beyond a few broad indications thus vouchsafed, Coleridge very astutely takes pains to avoid anything like geography. We reach that silent sea into which we are the first that ever burst, and that is sufficient for imaginative ends. It is enough that the world, as known to actual navigators, is left behind, and a world which the poet is free to colonize with the wildest children of his dreaming brain, has been entered. Forthwith, to all intents and purposes, we may say, in the words of Goethe as rendered by Shelley:

> "The bounds of true and false are passed; —
> Lead on, thou wandering gleam."

Thenceforth we cease to have any direct relations with the verifiable. Natural law is suspended; standards of probability have ceased to exist. Marvel after marvel is accepted by us, as by the Wedding-Guest, with the unquestioning faith of "a three years' child." We become insensibly acclimatized to this dreamland. Nor is it the chaotic, anarchic, incoherent world of arabesque romance, where the real and unreal by turns arbitrarily interrupt and supplant each other, and are never reconciled at heart. On the contrary, here is no inconsistency, for with the constitution of *this* dream-realm nothing except the natural and the probable would be inconsistent. Here is no danger of the intellect or the reason pronouncing an adverse judgment, for the venue has been changed to a court where the jurisdiction of fancy is supreme. Thus far then, the Logic of the Incredible is perfect, and the result, from the view point of art, magnificent. But at last we quit this consistently, unimpeachably, most satisfactorily impossible world; we are restored to the world of common experience; and when so restoring us, the poet makes his first and only mistake. For the concluding miracle, or rather brace of miracles — the apparition of the angelic forms standing over the corpses of the crew, and the sudden preternatural sinking of the ship — take place just when we have returned to the province of the natural and regular, to the sphere of the actual and the known; just when, floating into harbor, we sight the well-remembered kirk on the rock, and the steady weathercock which the moonlight steeps in silentness. A dissonant note is struck at once. We have left a world where prodigies were normal, and have returned to one where they are monstrous. But prodigies still pursue us with unseasonable pertinacity, and our feeling is somewhat akin to that of the Ancient Mariner himself, whose prayer is that he may either "be awake" or may "sleep alway." We would fain either surrender unconditionally to reality, or remain free, as naturalized citizens of a self-governing dreamland.

WILLIAM WATSON, *Excursions in Criticism*, pp. 98–101

And this poem is beyond question one of the supreme triumphs of poetry. Witness the men who brought batteries to bear on it right and left. Literally: for one critic said that the "moral sentiment" had impaired the imaginative excellence; another, that it failed and fell through for want of a moral foothold upon facts. Remembering these things, I am reluctant to proceed; but desirous to praise, as I best may. Though I doubt if it be worth while, seeing how *The Ancient Mariner*, praised or dispraised, lives and is like to live for the delight equally of young boys and old men; and seeing also that the last critic cited was no less a man than Hazlitt. It is fortunate, among many misfortunes, that for Coleridge no warning word was needed against the shriek of the press gang from this side or that. He stooped once or twice to spurn them; but he knew that he stooped. His intense and overwrought abstraction from things of the day or hour did him no ill service here.

The Ancient Mariner has doubtless more of breadth and space, more of material force and motion, than anything else of the poet's. And the tenderness of sentiment which touches with significant color the pure white imagination is here no longer morbid or languid, as in the earlier

poems of feeling and emotion. It is soft and piteous
enough, but womanly rather than effeminate; and thus
serves indeed to set off the strange splendors and bound-
less beauties of the story. For the execution, I presume
no human eye is too dull to see how perfect it is, and how
high in kind of perfection. Here is not the speckless
and elaborate finish which shows everywhere the fresh
rasp of file or chisel on its smooth and spruce excellence;
this is faultless after the fashion of a flower or a tree.
Thus it has grown: not thus has it been carved.

Swinburne, Essays and Studies, pp. 263, 264

*   *   *

It is enough for us here that he [Coleridge] has written
some of the most poetical poetry in the language, and one
poem, *The Ancient Mariner*, not only unparalleled, but
unapproached in its kind, and that kind of the rarest. It
is marvellous in the mastery over that delightfully fortui-
tous inconsequence that is the adamantine logic of dreamland. Coleridge has taken the old ballad measure and
given to it by indefinable charm wholly his own all
the sweetness, all the melody and compass of a symphony.
And how picturesque it is in the proper sense of the word.
I know nothing like it. There is not a description in it.
It is all picture. Descriptive poets generally confuse us
with multiplicity of detail; we cannot see their forest for
trees; but Coleridge never errs in this way. With instinc-
tive tact he touches the right chord of association, and is
satisfied, as we also are. I should find it hard to explain
the singular charm of his diction, there is so much nicety
of art and purpose in it, whether for music or for mean-

ing.   Nor does it need any explanation, for we all feel it.
The words seem common words enough, but in the order
of them, in the choice, variety, and position of the vowel
sounds they become magical.   The most decrepit vocable
in the language throws away its crutches to dance and sing
at his piping.   I cannot think it a personal peculiarity, but
a matter of universal experience, that more bits of Coleridge have embedded themselves in my memory than of
any other poet who delighted my youth—unless I should
except the sonnets of Shakespeare.   This argues perfect-
ness of expression.

LOWELL, Democracy and Other Addresses, pp. 98, 99

Christabel, though not printed till 1816, was written
mainly in the year 1797: *The Rhyme of the Ancient Mariner* was printed as a contribution to the *Lyrical Ballads* in
1798; and these two poems belong to the great year of
Coleridge's poetic production, his twenty-fifth year.   In
poetic quality, above all in that most poetic of all qualities,
a keen sense of, and delight in beauty, the infection of
which lays hold upon the reader, they are quite out of
proportion to all his other compositions.   The form in both
is that of the ballad, with some of its terminology, and
some also of its quaint conceits.   They connect themselves
with that revival of ballad literature, of which Percy's
Relics, and, in another way, Macpherson's *Ossian* are
monuments, and which afterwards so powerfully affected
Scott —

> " Young-eyed poesy
>   All deftly masked as hoar antiquity."

The Ancient Mariner . . . is a "romantic" poem, impressing us by bold invention, and appealing to that taste for the supernatural, that longing for *le frisson*, a shudder, to which the "romantic" school in Germany, and its derivations in England and France directly ministered. In Coleridge, personally, this taste had been encouraged by his odd and out-of-the-way reading in the old-fashioned literature of the marvellous—books like Purchas's *Pilgrims*, early voyages like Hakluyt's, old naturalists and visionary moralists, like Thomas Burnet, from whom he quotes the motto of *The Ancient Mariner*, "*Facile credo, plures esse naturas invisibiles quam visibiles in rerum universitate,*" *etc.* Fancies of the strange things which may very well happen, even in broad daylight, to men shut up alone in ships far off on the sea, seem to have occurred to the human mind in all ages with a peculiar readiness, and often have about them, from the story of the stealing of Dionysus downwards, the fascination of a certain dreamy grace, which distinguishes them from other kinds of marvellous inventions. This sort of fascination *The Ancient Mariner* brings to its highest degree: it is the delicacy, the dreamy grace, in his presentation of the marvellous, which makes Coleridge's work so remarkable. The too palpable intruders from a spiritual world in almost all ghost literature, in Scott and Shakespeare even, have a kind of crudity or coarseness. Coleridge's power is in the very fineness with which, as by some really ghostly finger, he brings home to our inmost sense his inventions, daring as they are — the skeleton ship, the polar spirit, the inspiriting of the dead corpses of the ship's crew. *The Rhyme of the Ancient Mariner* has the plausibility, the perfect adaptation to reason and the general aspect of life, which belongs to the marvellous, when actually presented as part of a credible experience in our dreams. Doubtless, the mere experience of the opium-eater, the habit he must almost necessarily fall into of noting the more elusive phenomena of dreams, had something to do with that: in its essence, however, it is connected with a more purely intellectual circumstance in the development of Coleridge's poetic gift. Some one once asked William Blake, to whom Coleridge has many resemblances, when either is at his best (that whole episode of the re-inspiriting of the ship's crew in *The Ancient Mariner* being comparable to Blake's well-known design of the " Morning Stars singing together "), whether he had ever seen a ghost, and was surprised when the famous seer, who ought, one might think, to have seen so many, answered frankly, " Only once ! " His " spirits," at once more delicate, and so much more real than any ghost — the burden, as they were the privilege, of his *temperament* — like it, were an integral element in his everyday life. And the difference of mood expressed in that question and its answer, is indicative of a change of temper in regard to the supernatural which has passed over the whole modern mind, and of which the true measure is the influence of the writings of Swedenborg. What that change is we may see if we compare the vision by which Swedenborg was " called," as he thought, to his work, with the ghost which called Hamlet, or the spells of Marlowe's *Faust* with those of Goethe's. The modern mind, so minutely self-scrutinizing, if it is to be affected at all by a sense of the supernatural, needs to be more finely touched than was possible in the older, romantic presentment of it. The spectral object, so crude, so impossible, has become plausible, as

> "The blot upon the brain
> That *will* show itself without;"

and is understood to be but a condition of one's own mind, for which, according to the skepticism, latent at least, in so much of our modern philosophy, the so-called real things themselves are but *spectra* after all.

It is this finer, more delicately marvellous supernaturalism, fruit of his more delicate psychology, that Coleridge infuses into romantic adventure, itself also then a new or revived thing in English literature; and with a fineness of weird effect in *The Ancient Mariner*, unknown in those older, more simple, romantic legends and ballads. It is a flower of medieval or later German romance, growing up in the peculiarly compounded atmosphere of modern psychological speculation, and putting forth in it wholly new qualities. The quaint prose commentary, which runs side by side with the verse of *The Ancient Mariner*, illustrates this — a composition of quite a different shade of beauty and merit from that of the verse which it accompanies, connecting this, the chief poem of Coleridge, with his philosophy, and emphasizing therein that psychological interest of which I have spoken, its curious soul-lore.

Completeness, the perfectly rounded wholeness and unity of the impression it leaves on the mind of a reader who fairly gives himself to it — that, too, is one of the characteristics of a really excellent work, in the poetic as in every other kind of art; and by this completeness, *The Ancient Mariner* certainly gains upon *Christabel* — a completeness, entire as that of Wordsworth's *Leech-gatherer*, or Keats's *Saint Agnes' Eve*, each typical in its way of such wholeness or entirety of effect on a careful reader. It is Coleridge's one great complete work, the one really finished thing, in a life of many beginnings. *Christabel* remained a fragment. In *The Ancient Mariner* this unity is secured in part by the skill with which the incidents of the marriage-feast are made to break in dreamily from time to time upon the main story. And then, how pleasantly, how reassuringly, the whole nightmare story itself is made to end, among the clear fresh sounds and lights of the bay, where it began, with

> The moonlight steeped in silentness,
> The steady weathercock.

WALTER PATER, *Appreciations*, pp. 96–101

If *The Ancient Mariner* is the finest example in our literature, of purely fantastic creation, — and we think it is, — the First Part of *Christabel* is not less wonderful in its power of producing an equally full and rich effect by infinitely more frugal means. In *Christabel*, there is nothing extravagant or bizarre, no mere imaginative libertinism, nothing that even most distantly suggests a riot of fancy. The glamour, everywhere present, is delicate, elusive, impalpable, curiously insidious, — the glamour of " enchantments drear, where more is meant than meets the ear." Acute critics seem to have felt from the first that the very essence of the unique attraction exercised by this poem lay in its obscurity, its enigmatical character, — that its fascination was preëminently the fascination of the impenetrable. Charles Lamb dreaded a " continuation " which should solve the riddle — and break the spell : which should light up — and destroy — this costly and faultless fabric of mystery. His fears (he was eventually reconciled to the "continuation" by the inimitable passage on divided friendship) were only too well justified. In the Second Part, Coleridge does not actually vulgarize his shadowland by letting in commonplace day-light; but he distinctly goes some little way in that direc-tion. It is not merely a falling-off in the quality of the workmanship — (although there *is* a falling-off of that sort, the poetry, as such, is still very fine) — but the whole basis, environment, and atmosphere of the First Part were magical, — and were homogeneous. The conditions of time and place were purely ideal ; there was no uncomfortable elbowing of Wonder by Familiarity ; the clumsy foot of Fact did not once tread upon the rustling train of Romance. But we turn to the continuation — we enter the second chamber of this enchanted palace — and we are met at the threshold by the dull and earthy imp, Topography. Since writing his First Part, Coleridge has removed to Keswick, and so, forsooth, when he resumes his story, we hear of Borrowdale and Langdale, of Bratha-Head and Dungeon-Ghyll. The sub-tlest part of the illusion is gone : the incursion of accidents has commenced, and the empire of fantasy is threatened. The notable thing is, that the point where the air of fine strangeness and aloofness ceases to be sustained, is precisely the point where the impression of *mere unreality* begins to make itself obtrusively felt. There has been conceded to us just that foothold in *terra firma* which affords a basis for the leisurely delimitation of *terra incognita*. And, truth to tell, the poet has not really taken up again his abandoned thread. How could he ? It was a filament of fairy gossamer, and he has endeavoured to piece it with what is, after all, only the very finest silk from the reel.

WILLIAM WATSON, *Excursions in Criticism*, pp. 101–103

Judging it . . . by any other standard than that of the poet's own erecting, one must certainly admit the claim of *Christabel* to rank very high as a work of pure creative art. It is so thoroughly suffused and permeated with the glow of mystical romance, the whole atmosphere of the poem is so exquisitely appropriate to the subject, and so marvellously preserved throughout, that our lack of belief in the reality of the scenes presented to us detracts but little from the pleasure afforded by the artistic excellence of its presentment. It abounds, too, in isolated pictures of sur-passing vividness and grace — word-pictures which live in the "memory of the eye" with all the wholeness and tenacity of an actual painting. Geraldine appearing to Christabel beneath the oak, and the two women stepping lightly across the hall "that echoes still, pass as lightly as you will," are pictures of this kind ; and nowhere out of Keats's *Eve of St. Agnes* is there any "interior" to match that of Christabel's chamber, done as it is in little more than half a dozen lines. These beauties, it is true, are fragmen-tary, like the poem itself, but there is no reason to believe that the poem itself would have gained anything in its entirety — that is to say, as a poetic narrative — by com-pletion. Its main idea — that the purity of a pure maiden is a charm more powerful for the protection of those dear to her than the spells of the evil one for their destruction — had been already sufficiently indicated.

H. D. TRAILL, *Coleridge*, p. 54

It is common to hear everything which Mr. Coleridge has written condemned with bitterness and boldness. His poems are called extravagant; and his prose works, poems too, and of the noblest breed, are pronounced to be mystical, obscure, theoretical, unintelligible, and so forth. . . . But *Christabel* is the only one of his writings which is ever treated with unmingled contempt; and I wish to examine with what justice this feeling has been excited. In the first place it should be remembered, that, at the time when it was written, the end of the last century, no attempt had been made in England by a man of genius for a hundred and fifty years to embody in poetry those resources which feudal manners and popular superstitions supply to the imagination. To those who care not for the mythology of demoniac terrors and wizard enchantment, Mr. Coleridge did not write, . . . but for those who, not believing the creed of the people, not holding that which was in great degree the substantial religion of Europe for a thousand years, yet see in these superstitions the forms under which devotion presented itself to the minds of our forefathers, the grotesque masque assumed for a period, like the veil on the face of Moses, as a covering for the glory of God. Persons who think this obsolete faith to be merely ridiculous, will of course think so of *Christabel*. He who perceives in them a beauty of their own, and discovers all the good to which in those ages they were necessary accompaniments, will not object to have them represented, together with all the attributes and associations which rightly belong to them, and in which genius, while it raises them from their dim cemetery, delights again to array them.

That much of the machinery of the poem is, in the eyes

of a natural philosopher or a woman of fashion, trivial or laughable, bears not upon the question. The fullest persuasion of the impossibility of every occurrence in the tale is not in the least incompatible with that kind of faith which is amply sufficient for the demands of the poet. It admits of much question, whether the mind be in the more healthy and natural state, when it is disposed to treat with scorn and ridicule whatever lies beyond the limit of its own convictions, or when it studies with affection and interest every shape and mode of human belief, and attempts to trace out and sympathize with that germ of good and truth, which lies somewhere amid the roots of every article of popular credence. But the latter is at all events the only condition of feeling on which poetry pretends to act; and he who brings a mind bristling with demonstration and experiment to receive the impact of a creative imagination, acts as iniquitously as Laertes fighting with a sword against the foil of Hamlet.

*   *   *

Throughout the poem there runs and lives one especial excellence, the beauty of single lines and expressions, perfect flowers in themselves, yet interfering as little with the breadth and unity of the general effect, as primroses and hawthorns of the valley with the sweeping perspective of light and shadow. No one, I imagine, can fail to recognize in it the original germ of *The Lay of the Last Minstrel;* but how superior is it to that spirited and brilliant tale, in the utter absence both of defect and superfluity in the diction, — in the thrilling interest and beauty of every, the slightest circumstance, — in the relation of each atom to the whole,

— and in the deep reflection, which is the very atmosphere and vital air of the whole composition!

JOHN STERLING, *Essays and Tales*, vol. i, pp. 101–103, 110
(reprinted from *The Athenæum*, 1828)

The former [*Kubla Khan*] is perhaps the most wonderful of all poems. In reading it we seem rapt into that paradise revealed to Swedenborg, where music and color and perfume were one, where you could hear the hues and see the harmonies of heaven. For absolute melody and splendor it were hardly rash to call it the first poem in the language. . . . All the elements that compose the perfect form of English metre, as limbs and veins and features a beautiful body of man, were more familiar, more subject, as it were, to this great poet than to any other.

SWINBURNE, *Essays and Studies*, p. 265

Facile credo, plures esse Naturas invisibiles quam visibiles in rerum universitate. Sed horum omnium familiam quis nobis enarrabit, et gradus et cognationes et discrimina et singulorum munera? Quid agunt? quæ loca habitant? Harum rerum notitiam semper ambivit ingenium humanum, numquam attigit. Juvat, interea, non diffiteor, quandoque in animo, tamquam in tabula, majoris et melioris mundi imaginem contemplari: ne mens assuefacta hodiernæ vitæ minutiis se contrahat nimis, et tota subsidat in pusillas cogitationes. Sed veritati interea invigilandum est, modusque servandus, ut certa ab incertis, diem a nocte, distinguamus.

T. BURNET, *Archæol. Phil.*, p. 68

THE RIME OF
THE ANCIENT MARINER

———◦◦◦———

PART I

It is an ancient Mariner,
And he stoppeth one of three.
"By thy long gray beard and glittering eye,
Now wherefore stopp'st thou me?

An ancient Mariner meeteth three gallants bidden to a wedding feast, and detaineth one.

5   "The Bridegroom's doors are opened wide,
And I am next of kin;
The guests are met, the feast is set:
May'st hear the merry din."

He holds him with his skinny hand,
10   "There was a ship," quoth he.
"Hold off! unhand me, graybeard loon!"
Eftsoons his hand dropt he.

He holds him with his glittering eye —
The wedding-guest stood still,
15   And listens like a three years' child:
The Mariner hath his will.

The wedding-guest is spellbound by the eye of the old seafaring man, and constrained to hear his tale.

The wedding-guest sat on a stone:
He can not choose but hear;
And thus spake on that ancient man,
20 The bright-eyed Mariner.

The ship was cheered, the harbor cleared,
Merrily did we drop
Below the kirk, below the hill,
24 Below the light-house top.

The Mariner
tells how the
ship sailed
southward
with a good
wind and fair
weather, till it
reached the
line.

The Sun came up upon the left,
Out of the sea came he!
And he shone bright, and on the right
Went down into the sea.

Higher and higher every day,
30 Till over the mast at noon —
The Wedding-Guest here beat his breast,
For he heard the loud bassoon.

The wedding-
guest heareth
the bridal
music; but the
Mariner con-
tinueth his
tale.

The bride hath paced into the hall,
Red as a rose is she;
Nodding their heads before her goes
The merry minstrelsy.

37 The Wedding-Guest he beat his breast,
Yet he can not choose but hear;
And thus spake on that ancient man,
40 The bright-eyed Mariner.

The ship
drawn by a
storm toward
the south
pole.

And now the Storm-blast came, and he
Was tyrannous and strong:
He struck with his o'ertaking wings,
And chased us south along.

The wedding-guest sat on a stone :
He can not choose but hear;

And thus spake on that ancient man,
The bright-eyed Mariner.

At length did cross an Albatross:
Thorough the fog it came;

As if it had been a Christian soul,
We hailed it in God's name.

45 With sloping masts and dipping prow,
  As who pursued with yell and blow
  Still treads the shadow of his foe,
  And forward bends his head,
  The ship drove fast, loud roared the blast,
50 And southward aye we fled.

  And now there came both mist and snow,
  And it grew wondrous cold ;
  And ice, mast-high, came floating by,
  As green as emerald.

55 And through the drifts the snowy clifts
  Did send a dismal sheen :
  Nor shapes of men nor beasts we ken —
  The ice was all between.

The land of ice and of fearful sounds, where no living thing was to be seen.

  The ice was here, the ice was there,
60 The ice was all around :
  It cracked and growled, and roared and howled,
  Like noises in a swound !

  At length did cross an Albatross :
  Thorough the fog it came ;
65 As if it had been a Christian soul,
  We hailed it in God's name.

Till a great seabird called the Albatross came through the snow-fog, and was received with great joy and hospitality.

  It ate the food it ne'er had eat,
  And round and round it flew.
  The ice did split with a thunder-fit ;
70 The helmsman steered us through !

And lo ! the Albatross proveth a bird of good omen, and followeth the ship as it returned northward through fog and floating ice.

And a good south wind sprung up behind ;
The Albatross did follow,
And every day, for food or play,
Came to the mariner's hollo !

In mist or cloud, on mast or shroud,
76 It perched for vespers nine ;
Whiles all the night, through fog-smoke white
Glimmered the white moon-shine.

The ancient Mariner inhospitably killeth the pious bird of good omen.

"God save thee, ancient Mariner !
From the fiends, that plague thee thus !—
Why look'st thou so?"—With my cross-bow
82 I shot the Albatross.

Part II

The Sun now rose upon the right :
Out of the sea came he,
85 Still hid in mist, and on the left
Went down into the sea.

And the good south wind still blew behind,
But no sweet bird did follow,
Nor any day for food or play
90 Came to the mariners' hollo !

His ship-mates cry out against the ancient Mariner, for killing the bird of good luck.

And I had done an hellish thing,
And it would work 'em woe :
For all averred, I had killed the bird
That made the breeze to blow.
95 Ah wretch ! said they, the bird to slay,
That made the breeze to blow !

Nor dim nor red, like God's own head,
The glorious Sun uprist:
Then all averred, I had killed the bird
100 That brought the fog and mist.
'T was right, said they, such birds to slay,
That bring the fog and mist.

The fair breeze blew, the white foam flew,
The furrow followed free;
105 We were the first that ever burst
Into that silent sea.

Down dropt the breeze, the sails dropt down,
'T was sad as sad could be;
And we did speak only to break
110 The silence of the sea!

All in a hot and copper sky,
The bloody Sun, at noon,
Right up above the mast did stand,
No bigger than the Moon.

115 Day after day, day after day,
We stuck, nor breath nor motion;
As idle as a painted ship
Upon a painted ocean.

Water, water, everywhere,
120 And all the boards did shrink;
Water, water, everywhere,
Nor any drop to drink.

The very deep did rot: O Christ!
That ever this should be!

But when the fog cleared off, they justify the same, and thus make themselves accomplices in the crime.

The fair breeze continues; the ship enters the Pacific Ocean, and sails northward, even until it reaches the Line.

The ship hath been suddenly becalmed.

And the Albatross begins to be avenged.

125 Yea, slimy things did crawl with legs
Upon the slimy sea.

About, about, in reel and rout
The death-fires danced at night;
The water, like a witch's oils,
130 Burnt green, and blue and white.

A spirit had followed them; one of the invisible inhabitants of this planet, neither departed souls nor angels;

And some in dreams assured were
Of the spirit that plagued us so;
Nine fathom deep he had followed us
From the land of mist and snow.

concerning whom the learned Jew, Josephus, and the Platonic Constantinopolitan, Michael Psellus, may be consulted. They are very numerous, and there is no climate or element without one or more.

135 And every tongue, through utter drought,
Was withered at the root;
We could not speak, no more than if
We had been choked with soot.

The shipmates in their sore distress would fain throw the whole guilt on the ancient Mariner; in sign whereof they hang the dead sea-bird round his neck.

Ah! well-a-day! what evil looks
Had I from old and young!
Instead of the cross, the Albatross
About my neck was hung.

PART III

There passed a weary time. Each throat
Was parched, and glazed each eye.
145 A weary time! a weary time!
How glazed each weary eye,
When looking westward, I beheld
A something in the sky.

The ancient Mariner beholdeth a sign in the element afar off.

At first it seemed a little speck,
150 And then it seemed a mist;
It moved and moved, and took at last
A certain shape, I wist.

A speck, a mist, a shape, I wist!
And still it neared and neared:
155 As if it dodged a water-sprite,
It plunged and tacked and veered.

With throats unslaked, with black lips baked,
We could not laugh nor wail;
Through utter drought all dumb we stood!
160 I bit my arm, I sucked the blood,
And cried, A sail! a sail!

At its nearer approach, it seemeth him to be a ship; and at a dear ransom he freeth his speech from the bonds of thirst.

With throats unslaked, with black lips baked,
Agape they heard me call:
Gramercy! they for joy did grin,
165 And all at once their breath drew in,
As they were drinking all.

A flash of joy;

See! see! (I cried) she tacks no more!
Hither to work us weal;
Without a breeze, without a tide,
170 She steadies with upright keel!

And horror follows. For can it be a ship that comes onward without wind or tide?

The western wave was all a-flame.
The day was well nigh done!
Almost upon the western wave
Rested the broad bright Sun;
175 When that strange shape drove suddenly
Betwixt us and the Sun.

It seemeth
him but the
skeleton of a
ship.

And straight the Sun was flecked with bars,
(Heaven's Mother send us grace!)
As if through a dungeon-grate he peered
180 With broad and burning face.

Alas! (thought I, and my heart beat loud)
How fast she nears and nears!
Are those her sails that glance in the Sun,
184 Like restless gossameres?

And its ribs
are seen as
bars on the
face of the set-
ting Sun.
The spectre-
woman and
her death-
mate, and no
other on board
the skeleton-
ship.

Are those her ribs through which the Sun
Did peer, as through a grate?
And is that Woman all her crew?
Is that a Death? and are there two?
Is Death that woman's mate?

Like vessel,
like crew!

190 Her lips were red, her looks were free,
Her locks were yellow as gold:
Her skin was as white as leprosy,
The Night-mare Life-in-Death was she,
194 Who thicks man's blood with cold.

Death and
Life-in-Death
have diced for
the ship's
crew, and she
(the latter)
winneth the
ancient
Mariner.

The naked hulk alongside came,
And the twain were casting dice;
"The game is done! I've won! I've won!"
Quoth she, and whistles thrice.

No twilight
within the
courts of the
Sun.

The Sun's rim dips; the stars rush out:
200 At one stride comes the dark;
With far-heard whisper, o'er the sea,
Off shot the spectre-bark.

We listened and looked sideways up !
Fear at my heart, as at a cup,
205 My life-blood seemed to sip !
The stars were dim, and thick the night,
The steersman's face by his lamp gleamed
     white ;
From the sails the dew did drip —
Till clomb above the eastern bar
210 The horned Moon, with one bright star
Within the nether tip.

At the rising of the Moon.

One after one, by the star-dogged Moon,
Too quick for groan or sigh,
Each turned his face with a ghastly pang,
215 And cursed me with his eye.

One after another,

Four times fifty living men,
(And I heard nor sigh nor groan)
With heavy thump, a lifeless lump,
They dropped down one by one.

His shipmates drop down dead ;

220 The souls did from their bodies fly, —
They fled to bliss or woe !
And every soul, it passed me by,
Like the whizz of my cross-bow !

But Life-in-Death begins her work on the ancient Mariner.

PART IV

" I fear thee, ancient Mariner !
225 I fear thy skinny hand !
And thou art long, and lank, and brown,
As is the ribbed sea-sand.

The wedding-guest feareth that a spirit is talking to him :

"I fear thee and thy glittering eye,
229 And thy skinny hand, so brown." —
Fear not, fear not, thou Wedding-Guest!
This body dropt not down.

But the ancient Mariner assureth him of his bodily life, and proceedeth to relate his horrible penance.

Alone, alone, all, all alone,
Alone on a wide wide sea!
And never a saint took pity on
235 My soul in agony.

He despiseth the creatures of the calm.

The many men, so beautiful!
And they all dead did lie:
And a thousand thousand slimy things
239 Lived on; and so did I.

And envieth that they should live, and so many lie dead.

I looked upon the rotting sea,
And drew my eyes away;
I looked upon the rotting deck,
And there the dead men lay.

I looked to Heaven, and tried to pray;
245 But or ever a prayer had gusht,
A wicked whisper came, and made
My heart as dry as dust.

I closed my lids, and kept them close,
And the balls like pulses beat;   [the sky
250 For the sky and the sea, and the sea and
Lay like a load on my weary eye,
And the dead were at my feet.

But the curse liveth for him in the eye of the dead men.

The cold sweat melted from their limbs,
Nor rot nor reek did they:

255 The look with which they looked on me
    Had never passed away.

An orphan's curse would drag to Hell
    A spirit from on high;
But oh! more horrible than that
260 Is a curse in a dead man's eye!
Seven days, seven nights, I saw that curse,
    And yet I could not die.

The moving Moon went up the sky,   *In his loneli-*
    And nowhere did abide: *ness and fixed-*
                                             ness he yearn-
265 Softly she was going up,   *eth towards*
    And a star or two beside —   *the journeying*
                                             Moon, and the
                                             stars that still
                                             sojourn, yet
                                             still move on-
ward; and everywhere the blue sky belongs to them, and is their appointed rest, and their native country and their own natural homes, which they enter unannounced, as lords that are certainly expected and yet there is a silent joy at their arrival.

Her beams bemocked the sultry main,
    Like April hoar-frost spread;
But where the ship's huge shadow lay,
270 The charmed water burnt alway
    A still and awful red.

Beyond the shadow of the ship,   *By the light of*
    I watched the water-snakes: *the Moon he*
                                               beholdeth
They moved in tracks of shining white,   *God's crea-*
275 And when they reared, the elfish light   *tures of the*
    Fell off in hoary flakes.   *great calm.*

Within the shadow of the ship,
    I watched their rich attire:
Blue, glossy green, and velvet black,
280 They coiled and swam; and every track
    Was a flash of golden fire.

Their beauty
and their hap-
piness.

O happy living things ! no tongue
Their beauty might declare :
284 A spring of love gushed from my heart,

He blesseth
them in his
heart.

And I blessed them unaware :
Sure my kind saint took pity on me,
And I blessed them unaware.

The spell be-
gins to break.

The selfsame moment I could pray ;
And from my neck so free
290 The Albatross fell off and sank
Like lead into the sea.

PART V

Oh sleep ! it is a gentle thing,
Beloved from pole to pole !
To Mary Queen the praise be given !
295 She sent the gentle sleep from Heaven,
That slid into my soul.

By grace of the
holy Mother,
the ancient
Mariner is re-
freshed with
rain.

The silly buckets on the deck,
That had so long remained,
I dreamt that they were filled with dew ;
300 And when I awoke, it rained.

My lips were wet, my throat was cold,
My garments all were dank ;
Sure I had drunken in my dreams,
And still my body drank.

305 I moved, and could not feel my limbs :
I was so light — almost

I thought that I had died in sleep,
And was a blessed ghost.

And soon I heard a roaring wind:
310 It did not come anear;
But with its sound it shook the sails,
That were so thin and sere.

He heareth strange sounds and seeth strange sights and commotions in the sky and the element.

The upper air burst into life!
And a hundred fire-flags sheen,
315 To and fro they were hurried about!
And to and fro, and in and out,
The wan stars danced between.

And the coming wind did roar more loud,
And the sails did sigh like sedge;
320 And the rain poured down from one black
     cloud;
The Moon was at its edge.

The thick black cloud was cleft, and still
The Moon was at its side:
Like waters shot from some high crag,
325 The lightning fell with never a jag,
A river steep and wide.

The loud wind never reached the ship,
Yet now the ship moved on!
Beneath the lightning and the moon
330 The dead men gave a groan.

The bodies of the ship's crew are inspired, and the ship moves on;

They groaned, they stirred, they all uprose,
Nor spoke, nor moved their eyes;
It had been strange, even in a dream,
To have seen those dead men rise.

335 The helmsman steered, the ship moved on;
      Yet never a breeze up blew;
      The mariners all 'gan work the ropes,
      Where they were wont to do;
      They raised their limbs like lifeless tools —
340 We were a ghastly crew.

      The body of my brother's son
      Stood by me, knee to knee:
      The body and I pulled at one rope,
344 But he said nought to me.

But not by the
souls of the
men, nor by
demons of
the earth or
midde air, but
by a blessed
troop of an-
gelic spirits,
sent down by the
invocation of the
guardian saint.

      " I fear thee, ancient Mariner!"
      Be calm, thou Wedding-Guest!
      'T was not those souls that fled in pain,
      Which to their corses came again,
      But a troop of spirits blest:

350 For when it dawned — they dropped their
            arms,
      And clustered round the mast;
      Sweet sounds rose slowly through their
            mouths,
      And from their bodies passed.

      Around, around, flew each sweet sound,
355 Then darted to the Sun;
      Slowly the sounds came back again,
      Now mixed, now one by one.

      Sometimes a-dropping from the sky
      I heard the sky-lark sing;

360 Sometimes all little birds that are,
How they seemed to fill the sea and air
With their sweet jargoning!

And now 't was like all instruments,
Now like a lonely flute;
365 And now it is an angel's song,
That makes the Heavens be mute.

It ceased; yet still the sails made on
A pleasant noise till noon,
A noise like of a hidden brook
370 In the leafy month of June,
That to the sleeping woods all night
Singeth a quiet tune.

Till noon we quietly sailed on,
Yet never a breeze did breathe:
375 Slowly and smoothly went the ship,
Moved onward from beneath.

Under the keel nine fathom deep,
From the land of mist and snow,
The spirit slid: and it was he
380 That made the ship to go.
The sails at noon left off their tune,
And the ship stood still also.

The lonesome spirit from the south pole carries on the ship as far as the line, in obedience to the angelic troop, but still requireth vengeance.

The Sun, right up above the mast,
Had fixed her to the ocean:
385 But in a minute she 'gan stir,
With a short uneasy motion —
Backwards and forwards half her length
With a short uneasy motion.

Then like a pawing horse let go,
390   She made a sudden bound:
It flung the blood into my head,
And I fell down in a swound.

How long in that same fit I lay,
I have not to declare;
But ere my living life returned,
I heard and in my soul discerned
Two voices in the air.

"Is it he?" quoth one, "Is this the man?
By him who died on cross,
With his cruel bow he laid full low
The harmless Albatross.

402   "The spirit who bideth by himself
In the land of mist and snow,
He loved the bird that loved the man
405   Who shot him with his bow."

The other was a softer voice,
As soft as honey-dew:
Quoth he, "The man hath penance done,
And penance more will do."

Part VI

First Voice

410   "But tell me, tell me! speak again,
Thy soft response renewing —
What makes that ship drive on so fast?
What is the Ocean doing?"

The Polar Spirit's fellow-demons, the invisible inhabitants of the element, take part in his wrong; and two of them relate, one to the other, that penance long and heavy for the ancient Mariner hath been accorded to the Polar Spirit, who returneth southward.

Second Voice

" Still as a slave before his lord,
415 The Ocean hath no blast ;
His great bright eye most silently
Up to the Moon is cast —

If he may know which way to go ;
For she guides him smooth or grim.
420 See, brother, see ! how graciously
She looketh down on him."

First Voice

" But why drives on that ship so fast,
Without or wave or wind ?"

The Mariner hath been cast into a trance ; for the angelic power causeth the vessel to drive northward faster than human life could endure.

Second Voice

" The air is cut away before,
425 And closes from behind.

" Fly, brother, fly ! more high, more high !
Or we shall be belated :
For slow and slow that ship will go,
When the Mariner's trance is abated."

430 I woke, and we were sailing on
As in a gentle weather :
'T was night, calm night, the Moon was high ;
The dead men stood together.

The supernatural motion is retarded ; the Mariner awakes, and his penance begins anew.

All stood together on the deck,
435 For a charnel-dungeon fitter :
All fixed on me their stony eyes,
That in the Moon did glitter.

The pang, the curse, with which they died,
Had never passed away :
440 I could not draw my eyes from theirs,
Nor turn them up to pray.

The curse is
finally expi-
ated.

And now this spell was snapt : once more
I viewed the ocean green,
And looked far forth, yet little saw
445 Of what had else been seen —

Like one, that on a lonesome road
Doth walk in fear and dread,
And having once turned round walks on,
And turns no more his head ;
450 Because he knows, a frightful fiend
Doth close behind him tread.

But soon there breathed a wind on me,
Nor sound nor motion made :
Its path was not upon the sea,
455 In ripple or in shade.

It raised my hair, it fanned my cheek
Like a meadow-gale of spring —
It mingled strangely with my fears,
Yet it felt like a welcoming.

460 Swiftly, swiftly flew the ship,
Yet she sailed softly too :
Sweetly, sweetly blew the breeze —
On me alone it blew.

And the an-
cient Mariner
beholdeth his
native country.

Oh! dream of joy! is this indeed
The light-house top I see ?

Is this the hill? is this the kirk?
Is this mine own countree?

We drifted o'er the harbor-bar,
And I with sobs did pray —
470 O let me be awake, my God!
Or let me sleep alway.

The harbor-bay was clear as glass,
So smoothly it was strewn!
And on the bay the moonlight lay,
475 And the shadow of the moon.

The rock shone bright, the kirk no less,
That stands above the rock:
The moonlight steeped in silentness
The steady weathercock.

480 And the bay was white with silent light,
Till rising from the same,
Full many shapes, that shadows were,
In crimson colors came.

> The angelic spirits leave the dead bodies,

A little distance from the prow
485 Those crimson shadows were:
I turned my eyes upon the deck —
Oh, Christ! what saw I there!

> And appear in their own forms of light

Each corse lay flat, lifeless and flat,
And, by the holy rood!
590 A man all light, a seraph-man,
On every corse there stood.

This seraph-band, each waved his hand:
It was a heavenly sight!
They stood as signals to the land,
495 Each one a lovely light;

This seraph-band, each waved his hand:
No voice did they impart —
No voice; but oh! the silence sank
Like music on my heart.

500 But soon I heard the dash of oars,
I heard the Pilot's cheer;
My head was turned perforce away,
And I saw a boat appear.

The Pilot and the Pilot's boy,
505 I heard them coming fast:
Dear Lord in Heaven! it was a joy
The dead men could not blast.

I saw a third — I heard his voice:
It is the Hermit good!
510 He singeth loud his godly hymns
That he makes in the wood.
He'll shrieve my soul, he'll wash away
The Albatross's blood.

Part VII

The Hermit of
the Wood,

This Hermit good lives in that wood
515 Which slopes down to the sea.
How loudly his sweet voice he rears!
He loves to talk with marineres
That come from a far countree.

This seraph-band, each waved his hand:
It was a heavenly sight!

They stood as signals to the land,
Each one a lovely light.

"Dear Lord! it hath a fiendish look —
(The Pilot made reply)
I am a-feared" — "Push on, push on!"
Said the Hermit cheerily.

He kneels at morn, and noon and eve —
520 He hath a cushion plump:
It is the moss that wholly hides
The rotted old oak-stump.

The skiff-boat neared: I heard them talk,
" Why, this is strange, I trow!
525 Where are those lights so many and fair,
That signal made but now?"

" Strange, by my faith!" the Hermit said — Approacheth
"And they answered not our cheer! the ship with
wonder.
The planks looked warped! and see those sails,
530 How thin they are and sere!
I never saw aught like to them,
Unless perchance it were

Brown skeletons of leaves that lag
My forest-brook along;
535 When the ivy-tod is heavy with snow,
And the owlet whoops to the wolf below,
That eats the she-wolf's young."

" Dear Lord! it hath a fiendish look —
(The Pilot made reply)
540 I am a-feared" — " Push on, push on!"
Said the Hermit cheerily.

The boat came closer to the ship,
But I nor spake nor stirred;
The boat came close beneath the ship,
545 And straight a sound was heard.

The ship sud-
denly sinketh.

Under the water it rumbled on,
Still louder and more dread :
It reached the ship, it split the bay ;
The ship went down like lead.

The ancient
Mariner is
saved in the
Pilot's boat.

Stunned by the loud and dreadful sound,
Which sky and ocean smote,
Like one that hath been seven days drowned
My body lay afloat ;
But swift as dreams, myself I found
555 Within the Pilot's boat.

Upon the whirl, where sank the ship,
The boat spun round and round ;
And all was still, save that the hill
Was telling of the sound.

560 I moved my lips — the Pilot shrieked
And fell down in a fit ;
The holy Hermit raised his eyes,
And prayed where he did sit.

I took the oars : the Pilot's boy,
565 Who now doth crazy go,
Laughed loud and long, and all the while
His eyes went to and fro.
"Ha ! ha !" quoth he, "full plain I see,
The Devil knows how to row."

570 And now, all in my own countree,
I stood on the firm land !
The Hermit stepped forth from the boat,
And scarcely he could stand.

" O shrieve me, shrieve me, holy man ! "
575 The Hermit crossed his brow.
" Say quick," quoth he, " I bid thee say —
What manner of man art thou ? "

The ancient
Mariner
earnestly en-
treateth the
Hermit to
shrieve him ;
and the pen-
ance of life
falls on him.

Forthwith this frame of mine was wrenched
With a woeful agony,
580 Which forced me to begin my tale ;
And then it left me free.

Since then, at an uncertain hour,
That agony returns :
And till my ghastly tale is told,
585 This heart within me burns.

And ever and
anon through-
out his future
life an agony
constraineth
him to travel
from land to
land,

I pass, like night, from land to land ;
I have strange power of speech ;
That moment that his face I see,
I know the man that must hear me :
590 To him my tale I teach.

What loud uproar bursts from that door !
The wedding-guests are there :
But in the garden-bower the bride
And bride-maids singing are :
595 And hark the little vesper-bell,
Which biddeth me to prayer !

O Wedding-Guest ! this soul hath been
Alone on a wide wide sea :
So lonely 't was, that God himself
600 Scarce seemed there to be.

O sweeter than the marriage-feast,
'T is sweeter far to me,
To walk together to the kirk
With a goodly company! —

605 To walk together to the kirk,
And all together pray,
While each to his great Father bends.
Old men, and babes, and loving friends,
And youths and maidens gay!

And to teach,
by his own
example, love
and reverence
to all things
that God made
and loveth.

Farewell, farewell! but this I tell
To thee, thou Wedding-Guest!
He prayeth well, who loveth well
Both man and bird and beast.

He prayeth best, who loveth best
615 All things both great and small;
For the dear God who loveth us,
He made and loveth all.

The Mariner, whose eye is bright,
Whose beard with age is hoar,
620 Is gone: and now the Wedding-Guest
Turned from the bridegroom's door.

He went like one that hath been stunned,
And is of sense forlorn:
A sadder and a wiser man,
625 He rose the morrow morn.

THE RIME OF

THE ANCYENT MARINERE

IN SEVEN PARTS

(Version of 1798)

———◦❖◦———

ARGUMENT

How a Ship having passed the Line was driven by Storms to the cold
Country towards the South Pole; and how from thence she made her
course to the Tropical Latitude of the Great Pacific Ocean; and of the
strange things that befell; and in what manner the Ancyent Marinere came
back to his own Country.

I

It is an ancient Marinere,
　　And he stoppeth one of three:
'By thy long grey beard and thy glittering eye
　'Now wherefore stoppest me?

5　　'The Bridegroom's doors are open'd wide,
　　'And I am next of kin;
'The Guests are met, the Feast is set, —
　'May'st hear the merry din.

But still he holds the wedding-guest —
10　　There was a Ship, quoth he —
'Nay, if thou 'st got a laughsome tale,
　'Marinere! come with me.'

He holds him with his skinny hand,
　　Quoth he, there was a Ship —

25

15 'Now get thee hence, thou grey-beard Loon!
'Or my Staff shall make thee skip.'

He holds him with his glittering eye —
　The wedding guest stood still
And listens like a three year's child;
20 　The Marinere hath his will.

The wedding-guest sate on a stone,
　He cannot chuse but hear;
And thus spake on that ancyent man,
　The bright-eyed Marinere.

25 The Ship was cheer'd, the Harbour clear'd —
　Merrily did we drop
Below the Kirk, below the Hill,
　Below the Light-house top.

The Sun came up upon the left,
30 　Out of the Sea came he:
And he shone bright, and on the right
　Went down into the Sea.

Higher and higher every day,
　Till over the mast at noon —
35 The wedding-guest here beat his breast,
　For he heard the loud bassoon.

The Bride hath pac'd into the Hall,
　Red as a rose is she;
Nodding their heads before her goes
40 　The merry Minstralsy.

The wedding-guest he beat his breast,
　Yet he cannot chuse but hear:
And thus spake on that ancyent Man,
　The bright-eyed Marinere.

45 Listen, Stranger ! Storm and Wind,[1]
   A Wind and Tempest strong !
  For days and weeks it play'd us freaks —
   Like Chaff we drove along.

  Listen, Stranger ! Mist and Snow,
50   And it grew wond'rous cauld :
  And Ice mast-high came floating by
   As green as Emerauld.

  And through the drifts the snowy clifts
   Did send a dismal sheen ;
55 Ne shapes of men ne beasts we ken —
   The Ice was all between.

  The Ice was here, the Ice was there,
   The Ice was all around :
  It crack'd and growl'd, and roar'd and howl'd —
60   Like noises of a swound.[2]

  At length did cross an Albatross,
   Thorough the Fog it came ;
  And an it were a Christian soul,
   We hail'd it in God's name.

65 The Marineres gave it biscuit-worms,
   And round and round it flew :

---

[1] The foot-notes show the changes made in the edition of 1800.

ll. 45–50. But now the Northwind came more fierce,
    There came a Tempest strong !
   And Southward still for days and weeks
    Like chaff we drove along.

   And now there came both Mist and Snow
    And it grew wondrous cold ;

[2] l. 60.   A wild and ceaseless sound.
    (The text of 1798 was afterwards restored.)

The Ice did split with a Thunder-fit,
  The Helmsman steer'd us thro'.

And a good south-wind sprung up behind,
70   The Albatross did follow;
And every day for food or play,
  Came to the Marinere's hollo!

In mist or cloud on mast or shroud,
  It perch'd for vespers nine,
75 Whiles all the night thro' fog-smoke white,
  Glimmer'd the white moon-shine.

' God save thee, ancyent Marinere!
  ' From the fiends that plague thee thus—
' Why look'st thou so?'— with my cross bow
80   I shot the Albatross.

II

The Sun came up upon the right,
  Out of the Sea came he;
And broad as a weft upon the left
  Went down into the Sea.

85 And the good south wind still blew behind,
  But no sweet Bird did follow
Ne any day for food or play
  Came to the Marinere's hollo!

And I had done an hellish thing
90   And it would work 'em woe:
For all averr'd I had kill'd the Bird
  That made the Breeze to blow.

Ne dim ne red, like God's own head,
  The glorious Sun uprist ;
95 Then all averr'd I had kill'd the Bird
  That brought the fog and mist.
'T was right, said they, such birds to slay
  That bring the fog and mist.

The breezes blew, the white foam flew,
100 The furrow follow'd free :
We were the first that ever burst
  Into that silent Sea.

Down dropt the breeze, the Sails dropt down,
  'T was sad as sad could be
105 And we did speak only to break
  The silence of the Sea.

All in a hot and copper sky
  The bloody sun at noon,
Right up above the mast did stand,
110 No bigger than the moon.

Day after day, day after day,
  We stuck, ne breath ne motion,
As idle as a painted Ship
  Upon a painted Ocean.

115 Water, water, every where,
  And all the boards did shrink ;
Water, water, everywhere,
  Ne any drop to drink.

The very deeps did rot : O Christ !
120 That ever this should be !
Yea, slimy things did crawl with legs
  Upon the slimy Sea.

About, about, in reel and rout,
   The Death-fires danc'd at night;
125 The water, like a witch's oils,
   Burnt green and blue and white.

And some in dreams assured were
   Of the Spirit that plagued us so;
Nine fathom deep he had follow'd us
130   From the Land of Mist and Snow.

And every tongue thro' utter drouth
   Was wither'd at the root;
We could not speak no more than if
   We had been choked with soot.

135 Ah! wel-a-day! what evil looks
   Had I from old and young;
Instead of the Cross the Albatross
   About my neck was hung.

III

I saw a something in the Sky,[1]
140   No bigger than my fist;
At first it seem'd a little speck
   And then it seem'd a mist:
It mov'd and mov'd, and took at last
   A certain shape, I wist.

145 A speck, a mist, a shape, I wist!
   And still it ner'd and ner'd;

[1] ll. 139, 140.   So past a weary time; each throat
               Was parch'd and glaz'd each eye,
          When, looking westward, I beheld
          A something in the sky.

And, an it dodg'd a water-sprite,
    It plung'd, and tack'd, and veer'd.

With throat unslack'd, with black lips bak'd
150   Ne could we laugh, ne wail:
Then while thro' drouth, all dumb they stood
I bit my arm and suck'd the blood
    And cry'd, A sail! a sail!

With throat unslack'd, with black lips bak'd,
155   Agape they hear'd me call;
Gramercy! they for joy did grin
And all at once their breath drew in
    As they were drinking all.

She doth not tack from side to side —
160   Hither to work us weal
Withouten wind, withouten tide,
    She steddies with upright keel.

The western wave was all a flame,
    The day was well nigh done!
165 Almost upon the western wave
    Rested the broad bright Sun;
When that strange shape drove suddenly
    Betwixt us and the Sun.

And strait the Sun was fleck'd with bars
170   (Heaven's mother send us grace)
As if thro' a dungeon grate he peer'd
    With broad and burning face.

Alas! (thought I, and my heart beat loud)
    How fast she neres and neres!
175 Are those *her* Sails that glance in the Sun
    Like restless gossameres?

Are those *her* naked ribs, which fleck'd
 The sun that did behind them peer?
And are those two all, all the crew,
180 That woman and her fleshless Pheere?

His bones were black with many a crack,
 All black and bare, I ween;
Jet-black and bare, save where with rust
Of mouldy damps and charnel crust
185 They're patch'd with purple and green.

Her lips are red, *her* looks are free,
 Her locks are yellow as gold:
Her skin is as white as leprosy,
And she is far liker Death than he;
190 Her flesh makes the still air cold.

The naked Hulk alongside came
 And the Twain were playing dice;
'The Game is done! I've won, I've won!'
 Quoth she, and whistled thrice.

195A gust of wind sterte up behind
 And whistled thro' his bones;
Thro' the holes of his eyes and the hole of his mouth
 Half-whistles and half-groans.

With never a whisper in the Sea
200 Off darts the Spectre-ship;
While clombe above the Eastern bar
The horned Moon, with one bright Star
 Almost atween the tips.

[1] ll. 177–180. Are those *her* Ribs, thro' which the Sun
     Did peer, as thro' a grate?
    And are those two all, all her crew,
     That Woman, and her Mate?

One after one by the horned Moon
 (Listen, O Stranger! to me)
Each turn'd his face with a ghastly pang
 And curs'd me with his ee.

Four times fifty living men,
 With never a sigh or groan,
With heavy thump, a lifeless lump,
 They dropp'd down one by one.

Their souls did from their bodies fly, —
 They fled to bliss or woe ;
And every soul it pass'd me by,
 Like the whiz of my Cross-bow.

IV

' I fear thee, ancyent Marinere !
 ' I fear thy skinny hand ;
' And thou art long, and lank, and brown,
 ' As is the ribb'd Sea-sand.

' I fear thee and thy glittering eye
 ' And thy skinny hand so brown.'—
Fear not, fear not, thou wedding guest !
 This body dropt not down.

Alone, alone, all all alone,
 Alone on the wide wide Sea ;
And Christ would take no pity on
 My soul in agony.

The many men so beautiful,
 And they all dead did lie !
And a million million slimy things
 Liv'd on — and so did I.

I look'd upon the rotting Sea,
   And drew my eyes away;
I look'd upon the eldritch deck,
235   And there the dead men lay.

I look'd to Heav'n, and try'd to pray;
   But or ever a prayer had gusht,
A wicked whisper came and made
   My heart as dry as dust.

240   I clos'd my lids and kept them close,
   Till the balls like pulses beat;
For the sky and the sea, and the sea and the sky,
Lay like a load on my weary eye,
   And the dead were at my feet.

245   The cold sweat melted from their limbs,
   Ne rot, ne reek did they;
The look with which they look'd on me,
   Had never pass'd away.

An orphan's curse would drag to Hell
250   A spirit from on high:
But O! more horrible than that
   Is the curse in a dead man's eye!
Seven days, seven nights I saw that curse,
   And yet I could not die.

255   The moving Moon went up the sky,
   And no where did abide:
Softly she was going up
   And a star or two beside —

Her beams bemock'd the sultry main
260   Like morning frosts yspread;

But where the ship's huge shadow lay,
The charmed water burnt alway
   A still and awful red.

Beyond the shadow of the ship
265   I watch'd the water-snakes:
They mov'd in tracks of shining white;
And when they rear'd, the elfish light
   Fell off in hoary flakes.

Within the shadow of the ship
270   I watch'd their rich attire:
Blue, glossy green, and velvet black
They coil'd and swam; and every track
   Was a flash of golden fire.

O happy living things! no tongue
275   Their beauty might declare:
A spring of love gusht from my heart,
   And I bless'd them unaware!
Sure my kind saint took pity on me,
   And I bless'd them unaware.

280 The self-same moment I could pray;
   And from my neck so free
The Albatross fell off, and sank
   Like lead into the sea.

v

O sleep, it is a gentle thing,
285   Belov'd from pole to pole!
To Mary-queen the praise be yeven
She sent the gentle sleep from heaven
   That slid into my soul.

The silly buckets on the deck
    That had so long remain'd;
I dreamt that they were fill'd with dew
    And when I awoke it rain'd.

My lips were wet, my throat was cold,
    My garments all were dank;
Sure I had drunken in my dreams
    And still my body drank.

I mov'd, and could not feel my limbs,
    I was so light, almost
I thought that I had died in sleep,
    And was a blessed Ghost.

The roaring wind! it roar'd far off,
    It did not come anear;
But with its sound it shook the sails
    That were so thin and sere.

The upper air bursts into life,
    And a hundred fire-flags sheen,
To and fro they are hurried about;
And to and fro, and in and out
    The stars dance on between.

The coming wind doth roar more loud;
    The sails do sigh, like sedge:
The rain pours down from one black cloud
    And the Moon is at its edge.

Hark! hark! the thick black cloud is cleft,
    And the Moon is at its side;
Like waters shot from some high crag,
The lightning falls with never a jag
    A river steep and wide.

The strong wind reach'd the ship : it roar'd
　　And dropp'd down, like a stone !
320 Beneath the lightning and the moon
　　The dead men gave a groan.

They groan'd, they stirr'd, they all uprose,
　　Ne spake, ne mov'd their eyes :
325 It had been strange, even in a dream
　　To have seen those dead men rise.

The helmsman steer'd, the ship mov'd on ;
　　Yet never a breeze up-blew ;
The Marineres all 'gan work the ropes,
330 　　Where they were wont to do :
They rais'd their limbs like lifeless tools —
　　We were a ghastly crew.

The body of my brother's son
　　Stood by me knee to knee :
335 The body and I pull'd at one rope,
　　But he said nought to me —
And I quak'd to think of my own voice [1]
　　How frightful it would be !

The day-light dawn'd — they dropp'd their arms,
340 　　And cluster'd round the mast :
Sweet sounds rose slowly thro' their mouths
　　And from their bodies pass'd.

Around, around, flew each sweet sound,
　　Then darted to the sun :
345 Slowly the sounds came back again
　　Now mix'd, now one by one.

[1] ll. 337, 338 omitted.

Sometimes a dropping from the sky,
　　I heard the Lavrock sing;
Sometimes all little birds that are
350　How they seem'd to fill the sea and air
　　With their sweet jargoning.

And now 't was like all instruments,
　　Now like a lonely flute;
And now it is an angel's song
355　　That makes the heavens be mute.

It ceas'd: yet still the sails made on
　　A pleasant noise till noon,
A noise like of a hidden brook
　　In the leafy month of June,
360　That to the sleeping woods all night
　　Singeth a quiet tune.

Listen, O listen, thou Wedding-guest ![1]
　　'Marinere! thou hast thy will:
'For that, which comes out of thine eye, doth make
365　　'My body and soul to be still.'

Never sadder tale was told
　　To a man of woman born;
Sadder and wiser thou wedding-guest!
　　Thou 'lt rise to-morrow morn.

370　Never sadder tale was heard
　　By a man of woman born:
The Marineres all return'd to work
　　As silent as beforne.

The Marineres all 'gan pull the ropes,
375　　But look at me they n'old:

[1] ll. 362–377. These four stanzas omitted.

Thought I, I am as thin as air—
  They cannot me behold.

Till noon we silently sail'd on
  Yet never a breeze did breathe:
380 Slowly and smoothly went the ship
  Mov'd onward from beneath.

Under the keel nine fathom deep
  From the land of mist and snow
The spirit slid: and it was He
385   That made the Ship to go.
The sails at noon left off their tune
  And the Ship stood still also.

The sun right up above the mast
  Had fix'd her to the ocean:
390 But in a minute she 'gan stir
  With a short uneasy motion—
Backwards and forwards half her length
  With a short uneasy motion.

Then, like a pawing horse let go,
395   She made a sudden bound:
It flung the blood into my head,
  And I fell into a swound.

How long in that same fit I lay,
  I have not to declare,
400 But ere my living life return'd,
I heard and in my soul discern'd
  Two voices in the air.

'Is it he?' quoth one, 'Is this the man?
  'By him who died on cross,

405   ' With his cruel bow he lay'd full low
        ' The harmless Albatross.

    ' The spirit who 'bideth by himself
        ' In the land of mist and snow,
    ' He lov'd the bird that lov'd the man
410   ' Who shot him with his bow.'

    The other was a softer voice,
        As soft as honey-dew :
    Quoth he the man hath penance done,
        And penance more will do.

VI

First Voice

415   ' But tell me, tell me ! speak again,
        ' Thy soft response renewing —
    ' What makes that ship drive on so fast ?
        ' What is the Ocean doing ? '

Second Voice

    ' Still as a Slave before his Lord,
420   ' The Ocean hath no blast :
    ' His great bright eye most silently
        ' Up to the moon is cast —

    ' If he may know which way to go,
        ' For she guides him smooth or grim.
425   ' See, brother, see ! how graciously
        ' She looketh down on him.'

First Voice

    ' But why drives on that ship so fast
        ` Withouten wave or wind ? '

SECOND VOICE

' The air is cut away before,
430   ' And closes from behind.

' Fly, brother, fly ! more high, more high,
    ' Or we shall be belated ;
' For slow and slow that ship will go,
    ' When the Marinere's trance is abated.'

435   I woke, and we were sailing on
    As in a gentle weather :
'T was night, calm night, the moon was high :
    The dead men stood together.

All stood together on the deck,
440   For a charnel-dungeon fitter :
All fix'd on me their stony eyes
    That in the moon did glitter.

The pang, the curse, with which they died,
    Had never pass'd away :
445   I could not draw my een from theirs
    Ne turn them up to pray.

And in its time the spell was snapt,
    And I could move my een :
I look'd far-forth, but little saw
450   Of what might else be seen.

Like one, that on a lonely road
    Doth walk in fear and dread,
And having once turn'd round, walks on
    And turns no more his head :
455   Because he knows, a frightful fiend
    Doth close behind him tread.

But soon there breath'd a wind on me,
    Ne sound ne motion made :
Its path was not upon the sea,
460   In ripple or in shade.

It rais'd my hair, it fann'd my cheek,
    Like a meadow-gale of spring —
It mingled strangely with my fears,
    Yet it felt like a welcoming.

465 Swiftly, swiftly flew the ship,
    Yet she sail'd softly too :
Sweetly, sweetly blew the breeze —
    On me alone it blew.

O dream of joy ! is this indeed
470   The light-house top I see ?
Is this the Hill ? Is this the Kirk ?
    Is this mine own countrée ?

We drifted o'er the Harbour-bar,
    And I with sobs did pray —
475 ' O let me be awake, my God !
    ' Or let me sleep alway ! '

The harbour-bay was clear as glass,
    So smoothly it was strewn !
And on the bay the moonlight lay,
480   And the shadow of the moon.

The moonlight bay was white all o'er,[1]
    Till rising from the same,
Full many shapes, that shadows were,
    Like as of torches came.

[1] ll. 481–502.   These five stanzas omitted.

485 A little distance from the prow
   Those dark-red shadows were ;
  But soon I saw that my own flesh
   Was red as in a glare.

  I turn'd my head in fear and dread,
490   And by the holy rood,
  The bodies had advanc'd and now
   Before the mast they stood.

  They lifted up their stiff right arms,
   They held them strait and tight ;
495 And each right-arm burnt like a torch,
   A torch that 's borne upright.
  Their stony eye-balls glitter'd on
   In the red and smoky light.

  I pray'd and turn'd my head away
500   Forth looking as before.
  There was no breeze upon the bay,
   No wave against the shore.

  The rock shone bright, the kirk no less
   That stands above the rock :
505 The moonlight steep'd in silentness
   The steady weathercock.

  And the bay was white with silent light,
   Till rising from the same
  Full many shapes, that shadows were,
510   In crimson colours came.

  A little distance from the prow
   Those crimson shadows were :
  I turn'd my eyes upon the deck —
   O Christ ! what saw I there ?

515   Each corse lay flat, lifeless and flat;
           And by the Holy rood,
       A man all light, a seraph-man,
           On every corse there stood.

       This seraph-band, each wav'd his hand:
520   It was a heavenly sight:
       They stood as signals to the land,
           Each one a lovely light:

       This seraph-band, each wav'd his hand,
           No voice did they impart —
525   No voice; but O! the silence sank,
           Like music on my heart.

       Eftsones I heard the dash of oars,
           I heard the pilot's cheer:
       My head was turn'd perforce away,
530   And I saw a boat appear.

       Then vanish'd all the lovely lights;[1]
           The bodies rose anew:
       With silent pace, each to his place,
           Came back the ghastly crew.
535   The wind, that shade nor motion made,
           On me alone it blew.

       The pilot, and the pilot's boy
           I heard them coming fast:
       Dear Lord in Heaven! it was a joy,
540   The dead men could not blast.

       I saw a third — I heard his voice:
           It is the Hermit good!
       He singeth loud his godly hymns
           That he makes in the wood.
545   He 'll shrieve my soul, he 'll wash away
           The Albatross's blood.

                    [1] ll. 531-536.   This stanza omitted.

VII

This Hermit good lives in that wood
 Which slopes down to the Sea.
How loudly his sweet voice he rears!
550 He loves to talk with Marineres
 That come from a far Countrée.

He kneels at morn and noon and eve —
 He hath a cushion plump:
It is the moss, that wholly hides
555 The rotted old Oak-stump.

The skiff-boat ne'rd: I heard them talk,
 ' Why, this is strange, I trow!
' Where are those lights so many and fair
 ' That signal made but now?'

560 ' Strange, by my faith!' the Hermit said —
 ' And they answer'd not our cheer.
' The planks look warp'd, and see those sails
 ' How thin they are and sere!
' I never saw aught like to them
565 ' Unless perchance it were

' The skeletons of leaves that lag
 ' My forest-brook along:
' When the Ivy-tod is heavy with snow,
' And the Owlet whoops to the wolf below
570 ' That eats the she-wolf's young.'

' Dear Lord! it has a fiendish look —
 (The Pilot made reply)
' I am afear'd ' — ' Push on, push on!'
 Said the Hermit cheerily.

575   The Boat came closer to the Ship,
           But I ne spake ne stirr'd !
       The Boat came close beneath the Ship,
           And strait a sound was heard !

       Under the water it rumbled on,
580   Still louder and more dread :
       It reach'd the Ship, it split the bay ;
           The Ship went down like lead.

       Stunn'd by that loud and dreadful sound,
           Which sky and ocean smote :
585   Like one that had been seven days drown'd
           My body lay afloat :
       But, swift as dreams, myself I found
           Within the Pilot's boat.

       Upon the whirl, where sank the Ship,
590   The boat spun round and round :
       And all was still, save that the hill
           Was telling of the sound.

       I mov'd my lips : the Pilot shriek'd
           And fell down in a fit,
595   The Holy Hermit rais'd his eyes
           And pray'd where he did sit.

       I took the oars : the Pilot's boy,
           Who now doth crazy go,
       Laugh'd loud and long, and all the while
600   His eyes went to and fro.
       ' Ha ! ha !' quoth he — 'full plain I see,
           ' The devil knows how to row.'

       And now all in mine own Countrée
           I stood on the firm land !

605   The Hermit stepp'd forth from the boat,
       And scarcely he could stand.

    'O shrieve me, shrieve me, holy Man!'
       The Hermit cross'd his brow —
    'Say quick,' quoth he, 'I bid thee say
610   'What manner man art thou?'

    Forthwith this frame of mine was wrench'd
       With a woeful agony,
    Which forc'd me to begin my tale
       And then it left me free.

615   Since then at an uncertain hour,[1]
       Now oftimes and now fewer,
    That anguish comes and makes me tell
       My ghastly aventure.

    I pass, like night, from land to land;
620   I have strange power of speech;
    The moment that his face I see
    I know the man that must hear me;
       To him my tale I teach.

    What loud uproar bursts from that door!
625   The Wedding-guests are there;
    But in the Garden-bower the Bride
       And Bride-maids singing are:
    And hark the little Vesper bell
       Which biddeth me to prayer.

---

[1] ll. 615–618.   Since then at an uncertain hour
        That agony returns;
      And till my ghastly tale is told
        This heart within me burns.

630   O Wedding-guest ! this soul hath been
            Alone on a wide wide sea :
        So lonely 't was, that God himself
            Scarce seemed there to be.

        O sweeter than the Marriage-feast,
635   'T is sweeter far to me
        To walk together to the Kirk
            With a goodly company.

        To walk together to the Kirk
            And all together pray,
640   While each to his great father bends,
        Old men, and babes, and loving friends,
            And Youths, and Maidens gay.

        Farewell, farewell ! but this I tell
            To thee, thou wedding-guest !
645   He prayeth well who loveth well,
            Both man and bird and beast.

        He prayeth best who loveth best,
            All things both great and small :
        For the dear God, who loveth us,
650   He made and loveth all.

        The Marinere, whose eye is bright,
            Whose beard with age is hoar,
        Is gone ; and now the wedding-guest
            Turn'd from the bridegroom's door.

655   He went, like one that hath been stunn'd
            And is of sense forlorn :
        A sadder and a wiser man
            He rose the morrow morn.

CHRISTABEL

'T is the middle of the night by the castle clock,
And the owls have awakened the crowing cock;
Tu — whit! —— Tu — whoo!
And hark, again! the crowing cock,
How drowsily it crew.   5

Sir Leoline, the Baron rich,
Hath a toothless mastiff bitch;
From her kennel beneath the rock
She maketh answer to the clock,
Four for the quarters, and twelve for the hour;   10
Ever and aye, by shine and shower,
Sixteen short howls, not over loud;
Some say, she sees my lady's shroud.

Is the night chilly and dark?
The night is chilly, but not dark.   15
The thin gray cloud is spread on high,
It covers but not hides the sky.
The moon is behind, and at the full;
And yet she looks both small and dull.
The night is chill, the cloud is gray: 20
'T is a month before the month of May,
And the Spring comes slowly up this way.

The lovely lady, Christabel,
Whom her father loves so well,
What makes her in the wood so late,   25
A furlong from the castle gate?
She had dreams all yesternight
Of her own betrothèd knight;
And she in the midnight wood will pray
For the weal of her lover that's far away.   30

She stole along, she nothing spoke,
The sighs she heaved were soft and low,
And naught was green upon the oak
But moss and rarest mistletoe:
She kneels beneath the huge oak tree,   35
And in silence prayeth she.

The lady sprang up suddenly,
The lovely lady, Christabel!
It moaned as near, as near can be,
But what it is, she cannot tell. —   40
On the other side it seems to be,
Of the huge, broad-breasted, old oak tree.

The night is chill; the forest bare;
Is it the wind that moaneth bleak?
There is not wind enough in the air   45
To move away the ringlet curl
From the lovely lady's cheek —
There is not wind enough to twirl
The one red leaf, the last of its clan,
That dances as often as dance it can,   50
Hanging so light, and hanging so high,
On the topmost twig that looks up at the sky.

Hush, beating heart of Christabel!
Jesu, Maria, shield her well!
She folded her arms beneath her cloak, 55
And stole to the other side of the oak.
   What sees she there?

There she sees a damsel bright,
Drest in a silken robe of white,
That shadowy in the moonlight shone: 60
The neck that made that white robe wan,
Her stately neck, and arms were bare;
Her blue-veined feet unsandal'd were;
And wildly glittered here and there
The gems entangled in her hair. 65
I guess, 't was frightful there to see
A lady so richly clad as she —
Beautiful exceedingly!

" Mary, mother, save me now!"
(Said Christabel) "and who art thou?" 70

The lady strange made answer meet,
And her voice was faint and sweet: —
" Have pity on my sore distress,
I scarce can speak for weariness:"
" Stretch forth thy hand, and have no fear!" 75
Said Christabel, " How camest thou here?"
And the lady, whose voice was faint and sweet,
Did thus pursue her answer meet: —

" My sire is of a noble line,
And my name is Geraldine: 80
Five warriors seized me yestermorn,
Me, even me, a maid forlorn:

They choked my cries with force and fright,
And tied me on a palfrey white.
The palfrey was as fleet as wind,   85
And they rode furiously behind.
They spurred amain, their steeds were white:
And once we crossed the shade of night.
As sure as Heaven shall rescue me,
I have no thought what men they be;   90
Nor do I know how long it is
(For I have lain entranced I wis)
Since one, the tallest of the five,
Took me from the palfrey's back,
A weary woman, scarce alive.   95
Some muttered words his comrades spoke:
He placed me underneath this oak;
He swore they would return with haste;
Whither they went I cannot tell —
I thought I heard, some minutes past,   100
Sounds as of a castle bell.
Stretch forth thy hand" (thus ended she)
"And help a wretched maid to flee."

Then Christabel stretched forth her hand,
And comforted fair Geraldine: 105
" O well, bright dame! may you command
The service of Sir Leoline;
And gladly our stout chivalry
Will he send forth and friends withal
To guide and guard you safe and free   110
Home to your noble father's hall."

She rose: and forth with steps they passed
That strove to be, and were not, fast.

Her gracious stars the lady blest,
And thus spake on sweet Christabel · 115
"All our household are at rest,
The hall as silent as the cell ;
Sir Leoline is weak in health,
And may not well awakened be,
But we will move as if in stealth, 120
And I beseech your courtesy,
This night, to share your couch with me."

They crossed the moat, and Christabel
Took the key that fitted well ;
A little door she opened straight, 125
All in the middle of the gate ;
The gate that was ironed within and without,
Where an army in battle array had marched out.
The lady sank, belike through pain,
And Christabel with might and main 130
Lifted her up, a weary weight,
Over the threshold of the gate :
Then the lady rose again,
And moved, as she were not in pain.

So free from danger, free from fear, 135
They crossed the court : right glad they were.
And Christabel devoutly cried
To the lady by her side,
"Praise we the Virgin all divine
Who hath rescued thee from thy distress !" 140
"Alas, alas !" said Geraldine,
"I cannot speak for weariness."
So free from danger, free from fear,
They crossed the court : right glad they were.

Outside her kennel, the mastiff old   145
Lay fast asleep, in moonshine cold.
The mastiff old did not awake,
Yet she an angry moan did make!
And what can ail the mastiff bitch?
Never till now she uttered yell   150
Beneath the eye of Christabel.
Perhaps it is the owlet's scritch:
For what can ail the mastiff bitch?

They passed the hall, that echoes still,
Pass as lightly as you will!   155
The brands were flat, the brands were dying,
Amid their own white ashes lying;
But when the lady passed, there came
A tongue of light, a fit of flame;
And Christabel saw the lady's eye,   160
And nothing else saw she thereby,
Save the boss of the shield of Sir Leoline tall,
Which hung in a murky old niche in the wall.
" O softly tread," said Christabel,
" My father seldom sleepeth well."   165

Sweet Christabel her feet doth bare,
And jealous of the listening air
They steal their way from stair to stair,
Now in glimmer, and now in gloom,
And now they pass the Baron's room,   170
As still as death, with stifled breath!
And now have reached her chamber door;
And now doth Geraldine press down
The rushes of the chamber floor.

The moon shines dim in the open air
And not a moonbeam enters here.
But they without its light can see
The chamber carved so curiously,
Carved with figures strange and sweet,
All made out of the carver's brain,⁣ 180
For a lady's chamber meet:
The lamp with twofold silver chain
Is fastened to an angel's feet.

The silver lamp burns dead and dim;
But Christabel the lamp will trim. 185
She trimmed the lamp, and made it bright,
And left it swinging to and fro,
While Geraldine, in wretched plight,
Sank down upon the floor below.

" O weary lady, Geraldine, 190
I pray you, drink this cordial wine !
It is a wine of virtuous powers ;
My mother made it of wild flowers."

"And will your mother pity me,
Who am a maiden most forlorn ?" 195
Christabel answered — " Woe is me !
She died the hour that I was born.
I have heard the gray-haired friar tell
How on her death-bed she did say,
That she should hear the castle-bell 200
Strike twelve upon my wedding day.
O mother dear ! that thou wert here ! "
" I would," said Geraldine, "she were ! "

But soon with altered voice, said she —
"Off, wandering mother! Peak and pine!   205
I have power to bid thee flee."
Alas! what ails poor Geraldine?
Why stares she with unsettled eye?
Can she the bodiless dead espy?
And why with hollow voice cries she,   210
"Off, woman, off! this hour is mine —
Though thou her guardian spirit be,
Off, woman, off! 't is given to me."

Then Christabel knelt by the lady's side,
And raised to heaven her eyes so blue —   215
"Alas!" said she, "this ghastly ride —
Dear lady! it hath wildered you!"
The lady wiped her moist cold brow,
And faintly said, " 'T is over now!"

Again the wild-flower wine she drank: 220
Her fair large eyes 'gan glitter bright,
And from the floor whereon she sank,
The lofty lady stood upright:
She was most beautiful to see,
Like a lady of a far countrée.   225

And thus the lofty lady spake —
"All they who live in the upper sky,
Do love you, holy Christabel!
And you love them, and for their sake
And for the good which me befel,   230
Even I in my degree will try,
Fair maiden, to requite you well.

But now unrobe yourself ; for I
Must pray, ere yet in bed I lie."

Quoth Christabel, " So let it be ! " 235
And as the lady bade, did she.
Her gentle limbs did she undress,
And lay down in her loveliness.

But through her brain, of weal and woe,
So many thoughts moved to and fro, 240
That vain it were her lids to close ;
So half-way from the bed she rose,
And on her elbow did recline,
To look at the lady Geraldine.

Beneath the lamp the lady bowed, 245
And slowly rolled her eyes around ;
Then drawing in her breath aloud,
Like one that shuddered, she unbound
The cincture from beneath her breast :
Her silken robe, and inner vest, 250
Dropt to her feet, and full in view,
Behold ! her bosom and half her side ——
A sight to dream of, not to tell !
O shield her ! shield sweet Christabel !

Yet Geraldine nor speaks nor stirs ; 255
Ah ! what a stricken look was hers !
Deep from within she seems half-way
To lift some weight with sick assay,
And eyes the maid and seeks delay ;
Then suddenly, as one defied, 260
Collects herself in scorn and pride,

And lay down by the Maiden's side ! —
And in her arms the maid she took,
     Ah wel-a-day !
And with low voice and doleful look   265
These words did say :
" In the touch of this bosom there worketh a spell,
Which is lord of thy utterance, Christabel !
Thou knowest to-night, and wilt know to-morrow,
This mark of my shame, this seal of my sorrow ;   270
    But vainly thou warrest,
     For this is alone in
    Thy power to declare,
     That in the dim forest
    Thou heard'st a low moaning,   275
And found'st a bright lady, surpassingly fair ;
And didst bring her home with thee in love and in charity,
To shield her and shelter her from the damp air."

The Conclusion to Part the First

    It was a lovely sight to see
    The lady Christabel, when she   280
    Was praying at the old oak tree.
     Amid the jagged shadows
     Of mossy leafless boughs,
     Kneeling in the moonlight,
     To make her gentle vows ;   285
    Her slender palms together prest,
    Heaving sometimes on her breast ;
    Her face resigned to bliss or bale —
    Her face, oh call it fair, not pale,

And both blue eyes more bright than clear,   290
Each about to have a tear.

With open eyes (ah woe is me!)
Asleep, and dreaming fearfully,
Fearfully dreaming, yet, I wis,
Dreaming that alone, which is —   295
O sorrow and shame! Can this be she,
The lady, who knelt at the old oak tree?
And lo! the worker of these harms,
That holds the maiden in her arms,
Seems to slumber still and mild,   300
As a mother with her child.

A star hath set, a star hath risen,
O Geraldine! since arms of thine
Have been the lovely lady's prison.
O Geraldine! one hour was thine —   305
Thou'st had thy will! By tairn and rill,
The night birds all that hour were still.
But now they are jubilant anew,
From cliff and tower, tu—whoo! tu—whoo!
Tu—whoo! tu—whoo! from wood and fell!   310

And see! the lady Christabel
Gathers herself from out her trance;
Her limbs relax, her countenance
Grows sad and soft; the smooth thin lids
Close o'er her eyes; and tears she sheds —   315
Large tears that leave the lashes bright!
And oft the while she seems to smile
As infants at a sudden light!

Yea, she doth smile, and she doth weep,
Like a youthful hermitess, 320
Beauteous in a wilderness,
Who, praying always, prays in sleep.
And, if she move unquietly,
Perchance, 't is but the blood so free
Comes back and tingles in her feet. 325
No doubt, she hath a vision sweet.
What if her guardian spirit 't were?
What if she knew her mother near?
But this she knows, in joys and woes,
That saints will aid if men will call: 330
For the blue sky bends over all!

Part the Second

"Each matin bell," the Baron saith,
"Knells us back to a world of death."
These words Sir Leoline first said,
When he rose and found his lady dead: 335
These words Sir Leoline will say
Many a morn to his dying day!

And hence the custom and law began,
That still at dawn the sacristan,
Who duly pulls the heavy bell, 340
Five and forty beads must tell
Between each stroke — a warning knell,
Which not a soul can choose but hear
From Bratha Head to Wyndermere.

Saith Bracy the bard, "So let it knell! 345
And let the drowsy sacristan
Still count as slowly as he can!

There is no lack of such, I ween,
As well fill up the space between."
In Langdale Pike and Witch's Lair,   350
And Dungeon-ghyll so foully rent,
With ropes of rock and bells of air
Three sinful sextons' ghosts are pent,
Who all give back, one after t'other,
The death-note to their living brother;   355
And oft too, by the knell offended,
Just as their one! two! three! is ended,
The devil mocks the doleful tale
With a merry peal from Borrowdale.

The air is still! through mist and cloud   360
That merry peal comes ringing loud;
And Geraldine shakes off her dread,
And rises lightly from the bed;
Puts on her silken vestments white,
And tricks her hair in lovely plight,   365
And nothing doubting of her spell
Awakens the lady Christabel.
" Sleep you, sweet lady Christabel?
I trust that you have rested well."

And Christabel awoke and spied   370
The same who lay down by her side —
O rather say, the same whom she
Raised up beneath the old oak tree!
Nay, fairer yet! and yet more fair!
For she belike hath drunken deep   375
Of all the blessedness of sleep!
And while she spake, her looks, her air,
Such gentle thankfulness declare,

That (so it seemed) her girded vests
Grew tight beneath her heaving breasts.   380
" Sure I have sinn'd ! " said Christabel,
" Now heaven be praised if all be well ! "
And in low faltering tones, yet sweet,
Did she the lofty lady greet
With such perplexity of mind   385
As dreams too lively leave behind.

So quickly she rose, and quickly arrayed
Her maiden limbs, and having prayed
That He, who on the cross did groan,
Might wash away her sins unknown,   390
She forthwith led fair Geraldine
To meet her sire, Sir Leoline.

The lovely maid and the lady tall
Are pacing both into the hall,
And pacing on through page and groom,   395
Enter the Baron's presence-room.

The Baron rose, and while he prest
His gentle daughter to his breast,
With cheerful wonder in his eyes
The lady Geraldine espies,   400
And gave such welcome to the same
As might beseem so bright a dame !

But when he heard the lady's tale,
And when she told her father's name,
Why waxed Sir Leoline so pale,   405
Murmuring o'er the name again,
Lord Roland de Vaux of Tryermaine ?

Alas ! they had been friends in youth ;
But whispering tongues can poison truth ;
And constancy lives in realms above ;   410
And life is thorny ; and youth is vain ;
And to be wroth with one we love
Doth work like madness in the brain.
And thus it chanced, as I divine,
With Roland and Sir Leoline.   415
Each spake words of high disdain
And insult to his heart's best brother :
They parted — ne'er to meet again !
But never either found another
To free the hollow heart from paining —   420
They stood aloof, the scars remaining,
Like cliffs which had been rent asunder ;
A dreary sea now flows between ; —
But neither heat, nor frost, nor thunder,
Shall wholly do away, I ween,   425
The marks of that which once hath been.

Sir Leoline, a moment's space,
Stood gazing on the damsel's face :
And the youthful Lord of Tryermaine
Came back upon his heart again.   430

O then the Baron forgot his age,
His noble heart swelled high with rage ;
He swore by the wounds in Jesu's side
He would proclaim it far and wide,
With trump and solemn heraldry,   435
That they, who thus had wronged the dame,
Were base as spotted infamy !
"And if they dare deny the same,

My herald shall appoint a week,
And let the recreant traitors seek   440
My tourney court — that there and then
I may dislodge their reptile souls
From the bodies and forms of men!"
He spake : his eye in lightning rolls!
For the lady was ruthlessly seized ; and he kenned   445
In the beautiful lady the child of his friend!

And now the tears were on his face,
And fondly in his arms he took
Fair Geraldine, who met the embrace,
Prolonging it with joyous look.   450
Which when she viewed, a vision fell
Upon the soul of Christabel,
The vision of fear, the touch and pain!
She shrunk and shuddered, and saw again —
(Ah, woe is me! Was it for thee,   455
Thou gentle maid! such sights to see?)

Again she saw that bosom old,
Again she felt that bosom cold,
And drew in her breath with a hissing sound :
Whereat the Knight turned wildly round,   460
And nothing saw, but his own sweet maid
With eyes upraised, as one that prayed.

The touch, the sight, had passed away,
And in its stead that vision blest,
Which comforted her after-rest,   465
While in the lady's arms she lay,
Had put a rapture in her breast,
And on her lips and o'er her eyes
Spread smiles like light!

With new surprise,
"What ails then my belovèd child?"   470
The Baron said — His daughter mild
Made answer, "All will yet be well!"
I ween, she had no power to tell
Aught else: so mighty was the spell.

Yet he, who saw this Geraldine,   475
Had deemed her sure a thing divine:
Such sorrow with such grace she blended,
As if she feared she had offended
Sweet Christabel, that gentle maid!
And with such lowly tones she prayed   480
She might be sent without delay
Home to her father's mansion.
                                        "Nay!
Nay, by my soul!" said Leoline.
"Ho! Bracy the bard, the charge be thine!
Go thou, with music sweet and loud,   485
And take two steeds with trappings proud,
And take the youth whom thou lov'st best,
To bear thy harp, and learn thy song,
And clothe you both in solemn vest,
And over the mountains haste along,   490
Lest wandering folk, that are abroad,
Detain you on the valley road.

"And when he has crossed the Irthing flood,
My merry bard! he hastes, he hastes
Up Knorren Moor, through Halegarth Wood,   495
And reaches soon that castle good
Which stands and threatens Scotland's wastes.

" Bard Bracy! bard Bracy! your horses are fleet,
Ye must ride up the hall, your music so sweet,
More loud than your horses' echoing feet!   500
And loud and loud to Lord Roland call,
' Thy daughter is safe in Langdale hall!
Thy beautiful daughter is safe and free —
Sir Leoline greets thee thus through me.
He bids thee come without delay,   505
With all thy numerous array,
And take thy lovely daughter home :
And he will meet thee on the way
With all his numerous array
White with their panting palfreys' foam :'   510
And, by mine honor! I will say,
That I repent me of the day
When I spake words of fierce disdain
To Roland de Vaux of Tryermaine! —
— For since that evil hour hath flown,   515
Many a summer's sun hath shone ;
Yet ne'er found I a friend again
Like Roland de Vaux of Tryermaine."

The lady fell, and clasped his knees,
Her face upraised, her eyes o'erflowing ;   520
And Bracy replied, with faltering voice,
His gracious hail on all bestowing! —
" Thy words, thou sire of Christabel,
Are sweeter than my harp can tell ;
Yet might I gain a boon of thee,   525
This day my journey should not be,
So strange a dream hath come to me,
That I had vowed with music loud

To clear yon wood from thing unblest,
Warned by a vision in my rest!　　　　　　　　530
For in my sleep I saw that dove,
That gentle bird, whom thou dost love,
And call'st by thy own daughter's name —
Sir Leoline! I saw the same
Fluttering, and uttering fearful moan,　　　　　535
Among the green herbs in the forest alone.
Which when I saw and when I heard,
I wonder'd what might ail the bird;
For nothing near it could I see,
Save the grass and green herbs underneath the old tree. 540

"And in my dream, methought, I went
To search out what might there be found;
And what the sweet bird's trouble meant,
That thus lay fluttering on the ground.
I went and peered, and could descry　　　　　545
No cause for her distressful cry;
But yet for her dear lady's sake
I stooped, methought, the dove to take,
When lo! I saw a bright green snake
Coiled around its wings and neck.　　　　　550
Green as the herbs on which it couched,
Close by the dove's its head it crouched;
And with the dove it heaves and stirs,
Swelling its neck as she swelled hers!
I woke; it was the midnight hour,　　　　　555
The clock was echoing in the tower;
But though my slumber was gone by,
This dream it would not pass away —
It seems to live upon my eye!

And thence I vowed this self-same day 560
With music strong and saintly song
To wander through the forest bare,
Lest aught unholy loiter there."

Thus Bracy said: the Baron, the while,
Half-listening heard him with a smile; 565
Then turned to Lady Geraldine,
His eyes made up of wonder and love;
And said in courtly accents fine,
" Sweet maid, Lord Roland's beauteous dove,
With arms more strong than harp or song, 570
Thy sire and I will crush the snake!"
He kissed her forehead as he spake,
And Geraldine in maiden wise,
Casting down her large bright eyes,
With blushing cheek and courtesy fine 575
She turned her from Sir Leoline;
Softly gathering up her train,
That o'er her right arm fell again;
And folded her arms across her chest,
And couched her head upon her breast, 580
And looked askance at Christabel ——
Jesu, Maria, shield her well!

A snake's small eye blinks dull and shy;
And the lady's eyes they shrunk in her head,
Each shrunk up to a serpent's eye, 585
And with somewhat of malice, and more of dread,
At Christabel she looked askance! ——
One moment — and the sight was fled!
But Christabel in dizzy trance

Stumbling on the unsteady ground   590
Shuddered aloud, with a hissing sound ;
And Geraldine again turned round,
And like a thing that sought relief,
Full of wonder and full of grief,
She rolled her large bright eyes divine   595
Wildly on Sir Leoline.

The maid, alas ! her thoughts are gone,
She nothing sees — no sight but one !
The maid, devoid of guile and sin,
I know not how, in fearful wise,   600
So deeply had she drunken in
That look, those shrunken serpent eyes,
That all her features were resigned
To this sole image in her mind :
And passively did imitate   605
That look of dull and treacherous hate !
And thus she stood, in dizzy trance,
Still picturing that look askance
With forced unconscious sympathy
Full before her father's view ——   610
As far as such a look could be
In eyes so innocent and blue !

And when the trance was o'er, the maid
Paused awhile, and inly prayed :
Then falling at the Baron's feet,   615
" By my mother's soul do I entreat
That thou this woman send away ! "
She said : and more she could not say :
For what she knew she could not tell,
O'er-mastered by the mighty spell.   620

Why is thy cheek so wan and wild,
Sir Leoline? Thy only child
Lies at thy feet, thy joy, thy pride,
So fair, so innocent, so mild;
The same, for whom thy lady died!   625
O by the pangs of her dear mother
Think thou no evil of thy child!
For her, and thee, and for no other,
She prayed the moment ere she died:
Prayed that the babe for whom she died,   630
Might prove her dear lord's joy and pride!
   That prayer her deadly pangs beguiled,
      Sir Leoline!
   And wouldst thou wrong thy only child,
      Her child and thine?   635

Within the Baron's heart and brain
If thoughts, like these, had any share,
They only swelled his rage and pain,
And did but work confusion there.
His heart was cleft with pain and rage,   640
His cheeks they quivered, his eyes were wild,
Dishonored thus in his old age;
Dishonored by his only child,
And all his hospitality
To the wronged daughter of his friend,   645
By more than woman's jealousy,
Brought thus to a disgraceful end —
He rolled his eye with stern regard
Upon the gentle minstrel bard,
And said in tones abrupt, austere —   650
"Why, Bracy! dost thou loiter here?

I bade thee hence ! " The bard obeyed ;
And turning from his own sweet maid,
The agèd knight, Sir Leoline,
Led forth the lady Geraldine !   655

The Conclusion to Part the Second

A little child, a limber elf,
Singing, dancing to itself,
A fairy thing with red round cheeks,
That always finds, and never seeks,
Makes such a vision to the sight   660
As fills a father's eyes with light ;
And pleasures flow in so thick and fast
Upon his heart, that he at last
Must needs express his love's excess
With words of unmeant bitterness.   665
Perhaps 't is pretty to force together
Thoughts so all unlike each other ;
To mutter and mock a broken charm,
To dally with wrong that does no harm.
Perhaps 't is tender too and pretty   670
At each wild word to feel within
A sweet recoil of love and pity.
And what, if in a world of sin
(O sorrow and shame should this be true !)
Such giddiness of heart and brain   675
Comes seldom save from rage and pain,
So talks as it 's most used to do.

KUBLA KHAN

In Xanadu did Kubla Khan
A stately pleasure-dome decree:
Where Alph, the sacred river, ran
Through caverns measureless to man
   Down to a sunless sea. 5
So twice five miles of fertile ground
With walls and towers were girdled round:
And there were gardens bright with sinuous rills
Where blossomed many an incense-bearing tree;
And here were forests ancient as the hills, 10
Enfolding sunny spots of greenery.

But oh! that deep romantic chasm which slanted
Down the green hill athwart a cedarn cover!
A savage place! as holy and enchanted
As e'er beneath a waning moon was haunted 15
By woman wailing for her demon-lover!
And from this chasm, with ceaseless turmoil seething,
As if this earth in fast thick pants were breathing,
A mighty fountain momently was forced:
Amid whose swift half-intermitted burst 20
Huge fragments vaulted like rebounding hail,
Or chaffy grain beneath the thresher's flail:
And 'mid these dancing rocks at once and ever
It flung up momently the sacred river.

Five miles meandering with a mazy motion　　25
Through wood and dale the sacred river ran,
Then reached the caverns measureless to man,
And sank in tumult to a lifeless ocean:
And 'mid this tumult Kubla heard from far
Ancestral voices prophesying war!　　30

　　The shadow of the dome of pleasure
　　Floated mid-way on the waves;
　　Where was heard the mingled measure
　　From the fountain and the caves.
It was a miracle of rare device,　　35
A sunny pleasure-dome with caves of ice!

　　A damsel with a dulcimer
　　In a vision once I saw:
　　It was an Abyssinian maid,
　　And on her dulcimer she played,　　40
　　Singing of Mount Abora.
　　Could I revive within me
　　Her symphony and song,
　　To such a deep delight 't would win me,
That with music loud and long,　　45
I would build that dome in air,
That sunny dome! those caves of ice!
And all who heard should see them there,
And all should cry, Beware! Beware!
His flashing eyes, his floating hair!　　50
Weave a circle round him thrice,
And close your eyes with holy dread,
For he on honey-dew hath fed,
And drunk the milk of Paradise.

NOTES

To the Teacher. The notes are intended to serve two distinct ends, explanation and appreciation. Concerning the use of the explanatory class, no question can arise; but the most profitable method of using the notes of the other class cannot be fixed for all pupils alike. It is not the editor's expectation that all the illustrative matter in this volume shall be mastered by every pupil; in many cases (some of which are indicated) it is expected that individual assignments will be made, in accordance with the tastes and abilities of pupils. In other cases it is plainly desirable that the teacher develop the suggestions made in the notes and report the result to the class. Some notes present themes for essays, others furnish topics more suitable for oral discussion. These directions apply also to the critical comments printed in the Introduction; they are embodied in the volume, not as authoritative judgments but as sources of suggestion and stimulus.

THE ANCIENT MARINER

(Heavy figures refer to pages, light figures to lines)

The motto. Following is a translation of the motto from Burnet:
I can well believe that there are in the Universe more invisible Beings than visible. But who shall reveal to us the family of them? or their degrees and relations and distinctions and several endowments? What do they? in what region do they dwell? The human mind has ever eagerly desired knowledge of these things, yet has never attained to it. In the meantime it is agreeable, I confess, to contemplate in the mind, as in a picture, the image of a grander and better world, lest the mind, wonted to the trivialities of everyday life, be narrowed overmuch and sink wholly into mean ideas. But at the same time we must have a care for the truth, and observe moderation, that we may distinguish between certainty and conjecture, day and night.

Rime. The derivation (Anglo-Saxon *rīm*; Middle English *rime*) shows this spelling to be etymologically correct rather than the ordinary form, *rhyme*, which is the result of a confusion beginning about 1550 between *rime* and *rhythm*. Usage has, of course, established the later form.

The gloss did not appear in the earliest editions; it was added in *Sibylline Leaves* (1817). What were Coleridge's motives for making this addition?

1 1 **It is an ancient Mariner:** a common form of introduction in the ballads.

1 3 **"By thy long gray beard":** Brandl regards this Turkish oath as an indication of the "eclectic tendency" of the Romantic school!

1 8 What is the subject of *may'st hear*?

1 12 **Eftsoons:** at once. (A.-S. *aeft* and *sōna*.)

1–2 13–19 Notice the mixed tenses. Cf. ll. 57–58, 363–365. Is this the result of carelessness?

1 15–16 These lines are Wordsworth's.

2 18 **He can not choose but hear:** "Doubtless this is a feature taken from life, for such a fascination did Coleridge himself exercise over his hearers." — Brandl

2 20 What is gained by putting the story into the mouth of the Ancient Mariner himself? Is there any advantage in his having the impatient wedding-guest as a listener? See Introduction, p. xxvi.

2 21 **The ship was cheered:** the ship was saluted with cheers. See New English Dictionary.

2 23 **kirk:** a Northern form of "church." Explain the presence of dialect words and archaisms in the poem.

2 21–24 What is the point of view — that of the Ancient Mariner on board the ship or that of an observer on shore?

2 34 **Red as a rose:** a very common comparison in the ballads.

2 36 **minstrelsy:** musicians.

3 47 **still:** constantly.

2–3 21–50 Do you agree with William Watson (see Introduction, p. xviii) that Coleridge shows "undignified haste to convey us to the æsthetically necessary region"?

3 45–50 Notice the definiteness of the imagery and the exquisite harmony between it and the tone of the poem.

3 55 **clifts:** clefts; see New English Dictionary under "cleft." It is also possible that *clifts* may mean *cliffs*. The Century Dictionary cites from Dryden a couplet in which the word is so used.

3 56 **sheen:** brightness. In l. 314 the word is used as an adjective.

3 57 **ken:** descry.

3 61 Notice the harmony between sound and sense.

3 62 **swound**: swoon.

3 64 **Thorough**: through. An archaism.

4 76 **vespers**: evenings.

4 77–78 Note both the intrinsic beauty of the treatment of light in these lines, and the part this treatment plays in constituting the atmosphere of the poem.

4 82 " The details were gathered from Shelvocke's *Voyage round the World*. He [Wordsworth] there read of a captain, by name Simon Hatley, a discontented, cruel, splenetic man. . . . The same, on a fearfully cold and stormy passage, far south of the Terra del Fuego, saw a black albatross, the only living thing in the wide waste of waters, who soared round and round the vessel for many days. The captain accordingly imagined in his superstitious way that the dark, disconsolate-looking bird had something to do with the bad weather, and in one of his gloomy fits shot the albatross, ' not doubting' (perhaps) ' that we should have a fair wind for it.' The guardian spirits of Nature, of whom Coleridge often sang in Stowey, revenged the murder ; and the ship's company agreed to put the mark of Cain on the criminal, by hanging the body of the albatross about his neck." — Brandl

4 92 **'em**: not colloquial, but archaic. (A.-S. *him*, dat. pl. of *hē*, *hit*, *hēo* ; M. E. *hem*.)

5 97 **like God's own head**: care should be taken in reading to connect this phrase with the latter part of the sentence.

5 98 **uprist**: this form occurs in Chaucer sometimes as a substantive, but usually as a third sing. pres. ind. (" upriseth "). It is here used by Coleridge as a third sing. pret. ind.

5 103–104 Alliteration.

5 104 **The furrow followed free**: in the edition of 1817 Coleridge changed this line to

> The furrow streamed off free.

His reason for doing so was that actual observation on board ship had taught him that the image described in the text is the one seen by a spectator from the shore or from another vessel, and that from the ship itself the wake appears like a brook flowing off from the stern. But in the later editions he restored the present reading. Which of the readings is preferable ?

5 117–118 Cf. *Hamlet*, II, ii, 501–504, when Pyrrhus' sword

> seemed i' the air to stick :
> So *as a painted tyrant*, Pyrrhus stood,
> And like a neutral to his will and matter
> Did nothing. (Hales)

6 128 death-fires : luminous appearances supposed to be seen over the places where dead bodies are buried. Cf. Coleridge's *Ode to the Departing Year*,

> Mighty armies of the dead
> Dance, like death-fires, round her tomb.

6 138 Notice the force of this homely comparison.

6 141 Five of the seven parts of the poem end with a reference to the Mariner's crime. Is this by accident or design? See l. 82, note.

7 152 I wist : this expression was probably conceived by Coleridge, and the ballad writers whom he imitated, to mean "I think," or "I guess." It is properly an adverb meaning "certainly." (A.-S. adj. *gewis* ; M. E. adv. *ywis, iwis*.) The two syllables being printed separately, the word was mistaken for a verb with subject pronoun. But cf. the Biblical expression "I wist" (I knew), which is regularly derived from the third sing. pret. ind. of the A.-S. verb *witan, wiste*.

7 149–161 Coleridge's imagination was stimulated by ships which he saw from the shore of the Bristol Channel, north of Stowey. Brandl makes the following reference to the matter : "He [Coleridge] was accustomed to wander of evenings on the shore to the north of Stowey, and watch a vessel emerging to sight on the open sea — first a little spot between himself and the setting sun ; then a dark little cloud ; then a shadowy form, mast and yards, black as iron crossbars ; while the solitary character of the coast helped to heighten the ghostly impression."

7 164 Gramercy ! An exclamation of gratitude or surprise (Fr. *grand merci*). — **grin :** "I took the thought of 'grinning for joy' . . . from poor Burnett's remark to me, when we had climbed to the top of Plinlimmon, and were nearly dead with thirst. We could not speak from the constriction, till we found a little puddle under a stone. He said to me, — ' You grinned like an idiot !' He had done the same." — Coleridge, *Table-Talk*, May 31, 1830

8 177–187 The skeleton ship was suggested to Coleridge by the dream of his friend Cruikshank.

8 184 gossameres : filmy cobwebs woven by small spiders.

8 197 "The game is done ! I've won ! I've won !" This is the reading of the editions of 1798 and 1800 and of most recent editions. Those of 1817, 1828, 1829, and 1834 read,

> The game is done ! I 've, I 've won !

In spite of this weight of authority and of the slightly increased emphasis on the pronoun, this reading is inferior, largely for a metrical reason.

8 198 **thrice**: a mystical number, much used in charms. Cf. Milton, *Comus*, ll. 914–915,

> Thrice upon thy finger's tip,
> Thrice upon thy rubied lip.

9 206–207 Notice the accuracy of the picture, especially of the light effects; consider the ghastly pallor of the steersman's face in the light of the binnacle, and the harmony between this detail and the tenor of the passage.

9 209 **clomb**: climbed. An archaism.

9 210–211 Is this imagination or observation? Is it ever possible to see a star within the tips of the moon?

9 226–227 "For the last two lines of this stanza I am indebted to Mr. Wordsworth. It was on a delightful walk from Nether Stowey to Dulverton, with him and his sister, in the autumn of 1797, that this poem was planned and in part composed." — Coleridge's note

11 263–266 Notice the contrast between the beauty of this stanza and the horrors of the narrative.

11 270 **charmed**: under a spell. (Lat. *carmen*, "a song," "an incantation.")

11 273 **water-snakes**: "In these monsters he [Coleridge] seems to have taken particular interest, and to have consulted various zoölogical works; for the note-book of this date contains long paragraphs upon the alligators, boas, and crocodiles of antediluvian times." — Brandl

12 282–291 Dowden comments: "That one self-centred in crude egoism should be purified and converted through a new sympathy with suffering and sorrow is a common piece of morality; this purification through sympathy with joy is a piece of finer and higher doctrine." — *New Studies in Literature*, p. 341

12 292–293 Cf. *The Pains of Sleep*,

> Sleep, the wide blessing.

12 295–296 Cf. Browning's *Christmas Eve*,

> Have I been sure, this Christmas Eve,
> God's own hand did the rainbow weave,
> Whereby the truth *from heaven slid*
> *Into my soul?*

12 297 **silly**: useless. Derived from A.-S. *sæl*, "time." The original meaning was "timely"; then "lucky," "happy," "blessed," "innocent," "simple," "foolish." Cf. Ger. *selig*.

13 314 **sheen**: bright. The use of this word as an adjective is archaic.

15 362 **jargoning**: *jargonner* is the usual word in Old French for the singing of birds.

14–15 354–372 Memorize.

15 385–388 Notice the skilful adaptation of the metre to the motion described.

16 404–405 " The consciousness of a central spirit of love and redemption is the religion of Coleridge's most vital poem, *The Ancient Mariner*."
— Vida D. Scudder, *The Life of the Spirit in the Modern English Poets*, p. 312

16 407 **honey-dew**: a sweet substance found in minute drops on the leaves of plants and trees. Cf. *Kubla Khan*, ll. 51–54.

17 435 **charnel-dungeon**: a vault for the deposit of dead bodies.

18 452 ff. "As the voyage approaches its conclusion, ordinary instrumentalities appear once more. There is first the rising of the soft familiar wind, 'like a meadow gale in spring,' then the blessed vision of the light-house top, the hill, the kirk, all those well-known realities which gradually relieve the absorbed excitement of the listener, and favor his slow return to ordinary daylight." — Mrs. Oliphant

18 460–463 Alliteration.

19 467 **countree**: an archaic form of "country," very common in the ballads.

19 472–479 Attempt to realize very definitely in your imagination the light and shade of this passage; compare this aspect with the corresponding aspect of earlier passages.

19 489 **rood**: cross.

20 492–495 Alliteration.

20 512 **shrieve**: hear confession and pronounce absolution.

21 521–522 Cf. *Christabel*, ll. 33–34.

21 524 **trow**: think, believe.

21 535 **ivy-tod**: ivy-bush. A dialect word.

22 549 See Introduction, p. xix.

22 560–569 Traill comments: "With what consummate art are we left to imagine the physical traces which the Mariner's long agony had left behind it, by a method far more terrible than any direct description — the effect, namely, which the sight of him produces upon others." — *Coleridge*, p. 52

24 610–617 " Mrs. Barbauld once told me that she admired *The Ancient Mariner* very much, but that there were two faults in it — it was improbable, and had no moral. As for the probability, I owned that that might admit some question; but as to the want of a moral, I told her that in my own judgment the poem had too much; and that the only or chief fault, if I might say so, was the obtrusion of the moral sentiment so openly on the reader as a principle or cause of action in a work of such pure imagination."
— Coleridge, *Table-Talk*, May 31, 1830

Mrs. Oliphant does not agree with Coleridge: "And then comes the ineffable half-childish, half-divine simplicity of those soft moralisings at the end, so strangely different from the tenor of the tale, so wonderfully perfecting its visionary strain. After all, the poet seems to say, after this weird excursion into the very deepest, awful heart of the seas and mysteries, here is your child's moral, a tender little half-trivial sentiment, yet profound as the blue depth of heaven. . . . This unexpected gentle conclusion brings our feet back to the common soil with a bewildered sweetness of relief and soft quiet after the prodigious strain of mental excitement which is like nothing else we can remember in poetry."— *Literary History of England, XVIIIth and XIXth Centuries*, vol. i, p. 249

CHRISTABEL

History. The First Part of *Christabel* was written at Nether Stowey in 1797, when the poetic genius of Coleridge was at its height. This Part bears traces of the observations of nature made by the author and by Dorothy Wordsworth in their walks in the region of Alfoxden and Nether Stowey. The Second Part was written at Keswick, in Cumberland, in 1800 — with the exception of the Conclusion, which was probably written in 1801. The Second Part contains many references to places in the Lake Country, some of which were visited by Wordsworth, his brother John, and Coleridge, in December, 1798. In the preface to the edition of 1816 Coleridge says that in his first conception of the tale the whole was present to his mind "with the wholeness no less than the liveliness of a vision." He then hoped to complete the "three Parts yet to come in the course of the present year." The hope of finishing the poem was abandoned late and reluctantly, for the author expressed it again in the prefaces of 1828 and 1829, and it was omitted only from the preface of 1834, a few months before Coleridge's death. In the meantime Coleridge repeatedly said that he had a plan for continuing the narrative and confessed that lack of inspiration or "poetic enthusiasm" alone prevented his doing so. In the *Table-Talk* of July 6, 1833, he asserts as his reason for finally abandoning the completion of *Christabel* the fact that continuations are almost inevitably failures.

Between its composition and its first publication (1816) *Christabel* circulated freely in manuscript. Copies were made by the author's friends, and the poem was widely discussed, so that it became almost as well known to the literary class as if it had been published. Indeed, it has the unusual distinction of having influenced notably the work of other poets years before its appearance in print. In 1804 Sir John Stoddart, a friend of

Scott, met Coleridge and heard him recite *Christabel*. He carried in his memory enough of the poem to give Sir Walter a notion of the metre and style. Scott was then in search of a suitable form for his minstrelsy and welcomed Coleridge's poem with delight, as giving him the very model for metre he desired. He attempted to use the metre in *The Lay of the Last Minstrel*, though with comparatively crude results. Byron also recognized the fitness of the metrical form for descriptive and narrative poetry and imitated it in a rejected opening for *The Siege of Corinth*.

Christabel was first published in 1816 (bound in a pamphlet with *Kubla Khan* and *The Pains of Sleep*) upon the recommendation of Byron, and by Byron's publisher, Murray. By many reviewers it was received contemptuously. An unsigned article in the *Edinburgh Review* was particularly offensive to Coleridge, because he attributed it to Hazlitt, who had been in youth a warm admirer. Although, in the main, the critics received the poem coldly, the poets were more discerning. In addition to Scott and Byron, Wordsworth, Shelley, Leigh Hunt, and Keats enthusiastically recognized its merit. The poets rather than the critics anticipated the judgment of posterity; the latter now seem ridiculous, the former prophetic.

Metre. In the preface of 1816 Coleridge describes the metre as follows : " The metre of *Christabel* is not, properly speaking, irregular, though it may seem so, from its being founded on a new principle, namely, that of counting in each line the accents, not the syllables. Though the latter may vary from seven to twelve, yet in each line the accents will be found to be only four. Nevertheless this variation in number of syllables is not introduced wantonly, or for the mere sake of convenience, but in correspondence with some transition in the nature of the imagery or passion." The freedom of the metre is a refinement of the same trait, as found in the popular Middle Age ballads, which in a sense served as models for *Christabel*. But the special motives of the artist appear in Coleridge's last sentence just quoted — *expression and variety*. No brief account can make clear the delicacy and power with which the poet has made the verse forms responsive to changes in his vision and feeling; but one example may suggest the flexibility and expressive power of the rhythms — Geraldine's words to Christabel at the end of Part I (ll. 267–270, especially). The entire speech contrasts sharply in content with all other passages in the First Part, being far more direct, intense, and dramatic. In these lines the metrical movement becomes almost regular, that is, the principle of counting syllables as well as accents may be applied to it. The metrical pattern is the anapæst, and the rhythm has a suggestion of stateliness appropriate to the situation.

In the touch| of this bos-| om there work|- eth a spell|
Which is lord| of thy ut-| terance Christ-| abel !|
Thou know-| est to-night| and wilt know| to-morrow|
This mark| of my shame,| this seal of | my sorrow.|

It is unwise to attempt formal scansion of English verse in school; but teachers should select several passages marked by expressive rhythms and encourage pupils to report similar passages.

49 1–22 Notice the triviality of the details. This was an offense to early critics. Can you account for it?

49 11 **Ever and aye, by shine and shower :** the first edition and several manuscripts read,

> Ever and aye, moonshine or shower.

Account for the revision.

49 14 **Is the night chilly and dark?** Compare ll. 25–26, 57, 149, 153, 207, 208, 209, 296–297, 327, 328, 403–407, 621–622. Is there any advantage in the question form?

49 14–22 Notice the characteristic atmosphere. This is Coleridge's "wizard twilight." For the most effective details of the description he may have been indebted to Dorothy Wordsworth. Her *Journal* of January 25, 1798, contains this entry : "... The sky spread over with one continuous cloud, whitened by the light of the moon, which, though her dim shape was seen, did not throw forth so strong a light as to chequer the earth with shadows." The entry of January 27 has atmospheric details that remind one of the first scene of *Christabel*. There is also mention of the howling of a "manufacturer's dog," which may possibly have been transformed into the mastiff bitch of the poem. The entry of March 27 presents other parallels.

50 32 First edition,

> The breezes they were still also ;

and one of the manuscripts,

> The breezes they were whispering low.

50 31–35 Notice the alliteration. Do you think it improves the passage?

50 31–36 John Sterling praises these lines as "beautiful specimens of a kind of excellence which runs through the whole poem, the presentation of the clearest and brightest pictures by the smallest number of words." — *Essays and Tales*, vol. i, p. 104

50 31–42 Notice the confusion of present and past tenses. Have you observed other examples? Can you account for it?

50 39 **It moaned as near, as near can be:** Why is the person to whom *it* refers so mysteriously introduced? Trace, as the tale progresses, the methods by which this mystery is disclosed.

50 45–52 Another example of wonderful description. Again it is possible that the author owed much to the sharp eyes of Dorothy Wordsworth. The entry in her *Journal* of March 7, 1798, contains this observation: " One only leaf upon the top of a tree — the sole remaining leaf — danced round and round like a rag blown by the wind."

51 58–68 This description of the strange lady was the result of a series of experiments. In Wordsworth's manuscript copy the passage reads,

> There she sees a damsel bright
> Clad in a silken robe of white,
> Her neck, her feet, her arms were bare
> And the jewels were tumbled in her hair.
> I guess, 't was frightful there to see
> A lady so richly clad as she, —
> Beautiful exceedingly.

And in several of the manuscripts the lines

> That shadowy in the moonlight shone,

and

> The neck, that made the white robe wan,

and

> Her blue-veined feet unsandal'd were

were omitted. Instead of lines 64, 65, there appeared in several manuscripts the single line,

> And the jewels disordered in her hair.

Compare these experimental forms and the version printed in the text.

51 66 **guess:** Is this word properly used? Cf. Chaucer, *Knight's Tale*, ll. 191–192,

> Hir yelow heer was broyded in a tresse
> Bihynde hir bak, a yerde long, I gesse.

51 69–70 The punctuation of *Christabel* has been conformed to the present standards in several particulars, even though variations from the early editions are involved. For example, in these lines and in several similar instances no marks of quotation are used in the editions that were prepared for the press by Coleridge himself. These changes are made for the sake of avoiding confusion.

51 71–103 Sterling comments: " Her [Geraldine's] narrative is a masterly counterfeiting of the effect which terror produces, in leading the sufferer to dwell on unimportant, as much as important details, and also exhibits the attempt which she makes, after the manner of all skilful liars, to add evidence to her story by minute details, together with the superfluity of epithets and adjuration, and shows her consciousness of falsehood by the overanxiety to secure credence. I am perfectly convinced that no play of our day by any other writer, — nor is this saying much, — contains a passage so dramatic as the tale told by Geraldine." — *Essays and Tales*, vol. i, p. 106

51 82 **forlorn:** quite lost. (A.-S. *forloren*; Ger. *verloren*.)

52 84 **palfrey:** a riding-horse, especially one suitable for a lady.

52 87 **amain:** energetically. (A.-S. *mægen*, " power," " might.")

52 92 See *The Ancient Mariner*, p. 7, l. 152, note.

52 108 **stout:** courageous.

52 112–122 In four of the manuscripts this passage reads,

> So up she rose and forth they pass'd
> With hurrying steps yet nothing fast.
> Her lucky stars the lady blest,
> And Christabel she sweetly said —
> All our household are at rest,
> Each one sleeping in his bed;
> Sir Leoline is weak in health
> And may not awakened be,
> So to my room we'll creep in stealth,
> And you to-night must sleep with me.

Carefully compare this reading with the text, and note and explain the substitutions and omissions.

53 117 **cell:** a small room, probably the lodging of a priest or monk.

53 123 **moat:** the defensive ditch surrounding a medieval castle.

53 125–126 **little door . . . all in the middle of the gate:** Why was not the gate itself open? Or why did not the lady unlock it?

53 129–136 The superstition that certain evil spirits may not enter one's dwelling except as drawn forcibly in by oneself is here brought into the story. It serves to indicate Geraldine's real character.

53 141–142 Why does not Geraldine respond to Christabel's proposal?

54 154–163 Study carefully the light and shadow of this interior. The fiction and poetry of the last quarter of the 18th century dealt much with the romantic interiors of castles. Walpole's *Castle of Otranto* had helped to create this taste. Scott's *Ivanhoe* and Keats's *Eve of St. Agnes* contain other examples of this phase of romanticism.

54 162 **boss:** a knob or projection in the centre of the shield.

55 175–183 Can you sketch the room from this description? Imagine the lighting, the walls, the furnishings and decorations. Would ampler details have made a more definite or pleasing picture? Compare this interior with those of Poe in *The Masque of the Red Death*, and that of Keats in *The Eve of St. Agnes*. In these comparisons consider not only the descriptions themselves but also their harmony with the narratives in which they appear.

55 191 **cordial :** tonic for the heart.

56 205 **Peak :** to become thin from illness. Cf. *Macbeth*, I, iii, 22–23,

> Weary se'nnights nine times nine,
> Shall he dwindle, peak, and pine.

56 221 **glitter :** wherein is the especial appropriateness of this word?

56 225 **Like a lady of a far countrée :** a phrase suggested by ballad literature. It is unusually appropriate in this poem, because it conveys the essence of romance, which Walter Pater defined as "strangeness added to beauty."

56 227–228 Bring together other passages and incidents that illustrate the nature of Christabel. Do you agree with Dowden that she has little character (in the sense of distinctive traits)?

57 252 **Behold !** The mysterious horror of Geraldine's person is left wholly to the imagination. This passage offers an opportunity of measuring the difference between Coleridge's appeal to the sense of horror and that of some of his contemporaries. For example, compare this passage of "Monk" Lewis's *Monk* : "She lifted up her veil slowly. What a sight presented itself to my startled eyes! I beheld before me an animated corpse!" — Quoted by Dowden, *New Studies in Literature*, p. 338

57 255–278 By what means is the First Part brought to a climax? By what metrical or rhetorical methods is the climax made impressive? Let some student be selected to present a carefully prepared study of the construction of the First Part, treating especially suspense and climax.

57 260–278 Consult the note on the metre (p. 82).

58 267 **a spell :** *Christabel*, although it is a poem in which the imagination works almost irresponsibly (or with responsibility only to its own laws), and deals with romantic and supernatural elements, still suggests delicately a moral mystery — that of the influence of an evil nature over a nature wholly innocent. These lines are the plainest indication of that influence. Trace the working of the spell in the succeeding Part.

59 306 **Tairn :** tarn. "Tairn or tarn . . . is properly a large pool or reservoir in the mountains, commonly the feeder of some mere in the valleys " (Note in one of Coleridge's manuscripts). See Wordsworth's description of Loughrigg Tarn in his *Guide to the Lakes*, in Grosart's edition of *The Prose Works of William Wordsworth*, vol. ii, p. 249. London, 1876.

59 310 **fell :** consult The Century Dictionary.

60 320 **hermitess :** a religious woman who has withdrawn from the world. Look up the origin and history of " hermit " in some standard dictionary.

60 332 **matin :** consult a dictionary.

60 339 **sacristan :** sexton ; in this case the sexton of the Baron's castle chapel.

60 341 **beads must tell :** every bead represented a prayer, which was counted to make up an assigned quota. Look up *tell*.

60 344 **Bratha Head, Wyndermere :** localities in the Lake Country. In William Sharp's *Literary Geography*, opposite page 168, is a picture of Windermere Lake. Wordsworth recommends the excursion from Ambleside, across the Bratha at Clappingsgate, and along the right bank of the Bratha to Skelwith-fold. For the congruity of these local references with the spirit of the poem, see William Watson's comments in the Introduction, p. xxvii.

60 346–347 **let the drowsy sacristan . . . count as slowly as he can :** this clause is concessive, meaning " However slowly the drowsy sexton may count." Cf. ll. 154–155.

61 350 **Langdale Pike :** Palmer's *English Lakes* has pictures of Windermere and of Langdale Pike, opposite page 28. "The solemn pikes of Langdale overlook, from a distance, the low cultivated ridge of land that forms the northern boundary of this small, quiet, and fertile domain " (Wordsworth, *Guide to the Lakes*, p. 249). Pike, a mountain or hill with a pointed summit. See New English Dictionary. See sketch by M. Greiffenhagen, in Sharp's *Literary Geography*.

61 351 **Dungeon-ghyll :** *ghyll* (gill) is a North-country word for a narrow valley, or ravine.

61 354 **Who all give back,** etc. : the echoes of bells among the hills are treated as of supernatural origin, probably in accordance with local superstition. Is this use of the supernatural harmonious with the First Part ?

61 365 **tricks :** dresses. — **plight :** braids.

61 375, 376 Cf. *The Ancient Mariner*, p. 12, ll. 292–293, and note ; cf. also Shakspere, *2 Henry IV*, III, i, 4–31.

63 408–426 " These lines, perhaps because they bring us out of the surrounding fairy-land, are the most famous in *Christabel* ; even the *Edinburgh* reviewer could see they were fine : ' We defy any man to point out a passage of poetical merit in any of the three pieces which it [the

Christabel pamphlet of 1816] contains, except, perhaps, the following lines in p. 32 [ll. 408–413], and even these are not very brilliant; nor is the leading thought original.'"— Note in Campbell's edition, p. 607. London and New York, 1895

The topic of estrangement between friends was doubtless suggested to Coleridge by his experiences with Charles Lloyd, Thomas Poole, and Lamb. "I suppose these lines leave almost every reader with a quickened sense of the beauty and compass of human feeling; and it is the sense of such richness and beauty which, in spite of 'dejection,' in spite of the burden of his morbid lassitude, accompanies Coleridge through life." — Pater, *Appreciations*, p. 102. London, 1890

63 435 **solemn heraldry :** formal proclamation by a herald, involving a challenge to the evil knights to submit to trial by battle. For this ordeal see Shakspere's *Richard II*, I, iii, and Scott's *Ivanhoe*, chap. 43.

64 445 **kenned :** recognized. Cf. Ger. *kennen*.

65 489 **solemn :** ceremonial. Cf. l. 435. Look up the derivation and history of the word in a standard dictionary.

65 496 **that castle good :** evidently Carlisle.

66 523–563 What is the relation between Bracy's dream and the main story ?

66 525 **boon :** look up the derivation of the word.

68 583–596 Compare with this passage, which suggests that Geraldine had the malignity of the serpent, the treatment of somewhat similar themes by Keats in *Lamia*, and by Dr. Holmes in *Elsie Venner*.

69 607–612 See l. 267 and note.

70 645 Several manuscripts and the editions of 1816, 1828, and 1829 read,

> To the insulted daughter of his friend.

71 656–677 Campbell thinks it highly improbable that these lines were originally intended as a part of *Christabel*. They were sent to Southey in a letter dated May 6, 1801, and were probably written in that year.

71 656–661 **A little child :** probably Coleridge's first child, Hartley, was the model for this cheerful picture. See Coleridge's sonnet *On receiving a Letter informing me of the Birth of a Son*, and Wordsworth's lines *To H. C.*

71 665 **unmeant bitterness :** The verses that follow present rather fine-drawn theories of " affectionate irony," or the practice of calling children " little rogues," " thieves," " old Turks," etc. Coleridge spoke slightingly of these theories of his, as unduly elaborate explanations of a simple matter; but they exemplify his remarkable bent for analyzing the workings of the mind and the heart; they bear the imprint of the " subtle-souled psychologist." Some of the theories suggest interesting principles of emphasis.

Conclusion. Coleridge felt it his duty to complete the tale, and did not abandon the hope of doing so until only a few months before his death. He asserted that he had a complete plan for the story of the Third, Fourth, and Fifth Parts, but could not master the necessary inspiration or "poetic enthusiasm." In Gillman's *Life* there appears a scheme for continuation that Coleridge had outlined to his friends. This "relation" may be found in Campbell's edition, p. 604. It is improbable that this plan was a part of Coleridge's original design or that he ever had a steadfast purpose of completing *Christabel* in accordance with this scheme, for Wordsworth, who was in Coleridge's confidence when the existing Parts were composed, knew nothing of any definite plan for completing the poem.

KUBLA KHAN

Origin. *Kubla Khan* was probably written in the summer of 1798, though the author dated it a year earlier. Coleridge had retired to a lonely farmhouse between Porlock and Linton, on the border of Somerset and Devonshire. As a result of an anodyne to which he had resorted for the relief of severe pain, he fell asleep over the pages of Purchas's *Pilgrimage*. He awoke some three hours later with a vivid consciousness of having composed not less than three or four hundred lines. "All the images rose up before him as *things*, with a parallel production of the correspondent expressions, without any sensation or consciousness of effort." His recollection of the entire vision was distinct, on awakening, and he began immediately to write it down. But he had written only the fifty-four lines that comprise the existing fragment, when he was interrupted by a "person from Porlock" who kept him in business conversation for an hour or more. When Coleridge was able to return to his writing, only a few scattered verses and dim images remained in his memory. He quotes from his own poem, *The Picture*, a description of the shattering of a reflected image when a stone is thrown into a pool:

> Then the charm
> Is broken — all the phantom world so fair
> Vanishes, and a thousand circlets spread,
> And each misshapes the other.

Source. The passage from Purchas which Coleridge was reading when he fell asleep follows:

"In Xamdu did Cublai Can build a stately Palace, encompassing sixteen miles of plaine ground with a wall, wherein are fertile Meadowes, pleasant Springs, delightfull Streames, and all sorts of beasts of chase and game and in the middest thereof a sumptuous house of pleasure." — *Purchas his Pilgrimage*, Book IV, chap. xiii. London, 1614

Publication. The fragment of *Kubla Khan* was first published by Murray, at the urgent instance of Byron, in a pamphlet with *Christabel* and *The Pains of Sleep*. The author justified the publication of it on the ground of psychological interest rather than poetic merit. This strange judgment has been reversed in both particulars : the experience of vivid dreams and of facile composition in dreams, as the result of some unusual condition of the brain, is by no means uncommon ; and on the other hand the sheer poetry is, in its own kind, not to be surpassed. Swinburne said that it is "perhaps the most wonderful of all poems," and his superlative may be understood even by those who cannot ratify it. Stevenson's *Chapter on Dreams* has interesting parallels to the author's experience.

72 1 Kubla Khan : Kublai Khan, a grandson of Jenghiz Khan, who was the founder of the Mongol dynasty. Kublai lived from about 1216 to 1294 ; he reigned over large parts of central Asia, China, and Russia ; he was a warrior, a patron of the arts and civilizer, a lover of splendor. *Khan* is a generic name, or title, meaning "supreme ruler."

72 1–5 In Stevenson's essay *On Some Technical Elements of Style in Literature* is a paragraph describing the pattern of letters that runs through these lines.

72 12 that deep romantic chasm : this exemplifies the romantic taste for wild scenery that grew up in the second half of the 18th century.

72 14–16 Kipling places these lines at "the high-water mark but two of the sons of Adam have reached,"—among the five supremely excellent lines in the poetry of the world. See "Wireless," in *Traffics and Discoveries*.

72 16 This line is used by Byron as a motto for his *Heaven and Earth*.

73 25–54 The blend of rhyme, rhythm, assonance, and alliteration in tne last half of the fragment reveals the hand of a supreme master of rhythms and verbal melodies.

73 30 This line is of wonderful beauty of sound.

73 46 that dome in air : this phrase is used by John Vance Cheney as the title of a volume of essays on poetry.

73 51–54 These verses are often applied to their author.